It's Been Fun!

The Story of
G.M. ("Mickey") Hajash

As Told to Gwen McLaws

Cover photo: Mickey trying out for the *Calgary Stampeders*, 1949.

PREFACE

This is the story of a five-year old Hungarian immigrant boy who began his life in Canada in a tar paper shack in Estevan, Saskatchewan, at the beginning of the Dirty Thirties and who went on from there to become a record-breaking athlete, a highly regarded geophysicist who travelled the world exploring for oil and who, in his retirement has devoted himself to philanthropy and other forms of community service.

What were the steps between, and could I tell his story? Initially, the Hajash's were hesitant. They were not keen on intrusion into their private lives. Michael, known to everyone as "Mickey" Hajash was afraid that he would come across as a braggart, or pompous, that his account of his life could seem to be self-serving. When he was eventually convinced that this was unlikely and appealed to on the grounds that this could be seen as a "family history", he agreed.

Armed with a recorder and tapes, he sat down to tell his story – and this he did with unsparing honesty. He displayed an amazing memory, a willingness to answer intrusive questions, a sly sense of humour and endless patience in explaining complexities.

After listening to the tapes, I decided to produce this informal "as spoken" memoir rather than a full-fledged biography of this man's life. The tapes were transcribed and the raw transcript was then lightly edited to make the spoken language more readable in print form without losing too much of the authentic Canadian prairie voice in which Mickey, despite all his worldly experience, continues (to his credit) to express himself.

My thanks to Donna Hajash for her patience with us and to their daughter Trish who, along with my daughter, Penny, rendered valuable assistance in the transcription of the tapes.

This effort would not have been possible without the help and encouragement of my brother, Ken, and wife, Natalie Rea, of Toronto. They have guided me every step of the way, and as writers themselves have provided the editing and advice necessary for me to put into print the story of this unusual man and his most unusual life.

Gwen McLaws
Victoria, B.C.
June 2006

CONTENTS

FIGURES

Figure 1: Mother, father and eldest brother Joe in Matramindszent.

Chapter 1 – Matramindszent to Estevan

Grayson Michael Hajas was born on May 6, 1924, in the village of Matramindszent, Heves Megye, Hungary, the third child of James and Kathrine (Kun) Hajas. In 1929 with his mother and two brothers he emigrated to Canada where they joined his father in Estevan, Saskatchewan. (The spelling of the family name was changed to Hajash after they settled in Canada.)

Matramindszent, Hungary

It is hard to recall the first memories of my life in Matramindszent, Hungary. I was five. I can remember the village and some of the things I did with my brothers because they were looking after me. Two brothers – Joe, four years older, and Jim, two and a half years older. The oldest kids had to look after the other kids. Joe and Jim and I would have chores to do, things like herding geese. In the evening we would bring the geese in and get them bedded down and then in the morning we'd take them out to feed along the roadside. The village, with a population of about 500 or so, was where everyone lived, as in feudal times, and all the land being worked lay outside the village. We lived in our grandfather's big house which was in the middle of the town.

My grandfather's name was Steven (I am using the Anglicized version of their names). He was born in 1878 and died in 1938. He was the mayor of the town so we were sort of the head household there – if there was such a thing. They had seven children. My father was the eldest son and helped his father, acting as a kind of foreman telling people what to do and how to do it. I think that was his main role. Of course, like everyone else, he had to serve two years in the army and he was away doing his military service when I was born.

My uncle Andy, Steven's third son, took over when my grandfather let the reins go and became the next mayor for many years. This was during the periods of German influence, the Second World War and the Russian invasion and, from what I saw (we visited Hungary in the 1960's, 70's and 80's), Andy did a pretty good job of handling a difficult situation with the occupation of his country. He was a very likeable fellow and you could see how he managed to please everyone. My uncle Steven, the fourth son, was captured in the war and was locked up in a Siberian prisoner-of-war camp. He returned, but died shortly thereafter.

My Mom was of the village – from a family of six. Very few girls married outside the village. There were many in town named Hajas – many clans. Her sister Rose married John Hajas (no relation) who was of the Hajas Hajas clan. I have translated ours as the "sheep" clan.

My mother would do her chores and look after us – feed us, clothe us, and then look after the other people in the house. There were a bunch of us in the house – lots of people, uncles and aunts. I'm not sure they all lived in the house, but I have a feeling they did. There could easily have been twelve there. I don't remember too much about the house except that in the center part there was a big stove with an oven that served as a heating plant and provided hot water for washing. The rest of the house was mainly bedrooms. I remember that with the big oven in the centre it got pretty hot in the summer so there was a summer kitchen outside. My recollection of what our meals were like is rather vague but I think we probably had the same kind of meals we had later on – cooked in the old-country way.

I think it was a happy household – at least while we were young, anyway. Later on, things happened which we'll talk about later, some very sad things. But I think that, for the most part, it was a happy household. Mom and Dad, I guess, were happy. Gabriel, the number two son, was married. The daughters probably weren't married at the time but I think Grandma was a pretty nice lady and the household seemed to run pretty well.

Much of the land and a lot of the forest in the area were still in the hands of large landholders but, by the time we're talking about, many of the common people also owned some land. I remember reading that our family had 70 hectares. Mom's family had 80 hectares which was a lot of land in that part of the country. They grew wheat and barley. I don't know about rye. I can't remember cattle but they must have had some – for the milk. There must have been a hog or two because they had to feed that big family and no doubt did their own raising and butchering.

They also grew flax, I know. They grew it, harvested it, spun it, and then wove the thread into cloth. This was the main clothing we wore. We were self-sufficient, I believe.

The women worked in the fields alongside the men or in groups of their own. When they had babies, they took only a few days off before they were back at work. Babies were taken care of by whoever was left in the house. Some were sisters or other relatives of the family, and kids like me were looked after by their older brothers. The girls had their jobs, mainly looking after the very young babies. Come feeding time they would take them out to the fields to the mothers. Everybody had a job to do and I guess the point I am trying to make is that the women worked pretty darn hard alongside the men.

3

We were Roman Catholic – everybody was. The family was quite religious but my grandfather was a bit of a drinker and so was my dad. I don't know how religious they were, but Mom went to church regularly and I think we were considered good Catholics.

Father had maybe grade three or four by way of education. He always said he had "bad eyes" which may have been an excuse for not having gone further in school. The emphasis obviously was on work and chores. Education was not considered too important. Mother may have had a bit more, but I'm not sure how much.

Brother Joe went to school there and Jim was just starting.

Why did my father leave? I don't know the details. I never really asked but I would guess it was Dad's outlook for the future of his family. As generations came and went, everything was shrinking and, as property was subdivided, the fields got narrower and narrower. I remember one guy saying their land had got so small they could step across their inheritance. So I believe my father thought there was a better life waiting in Canada. He had heard all kinds of rumours about how nice it was in Canada – this was in the late 1920's when things were really roaring there.

I believe a few of the villagers had gone to Canada and come back home and, of course, through word of mouth, news got around about how nice it was. Yes, I think a lot of them also went to the States. So it was either the States or Canada. My father went to Canada in 1927 and worked in the lignite coal mines at Estevan in southern Saskatchewan on and off for two years. I think he had some friends that had gone there. He wasn't a miner but he was a strong young guy and he worked all around Roche Perce and

Bienfait – wherever he could get work. There was also a pottery factory and he would work summers there and at the coal mines in winter.

He worked and saved enough to bring us out to Canada. It was in 1929 that Mother and we three boys came out.

I remember leaving Hungary but only vaguely. There was only one car in our village and that belonged to the doctor. I recall going through Budapest but I don't know how we got there. I think we spent only a few days there but I sure remember the Underground which I believe was the first to have been built in Europe. I remember that somehow I missed following the family when we were walking and got lost for a few hours. Anyway, they finally found me and I guess we took a train to Antwerp. I remember boarding an old liner. And we arrived in St. John, New Brunswick.

I remember the sea trip only vaguely. We all suffered various degrees of sea sickness and Mother spent a lot of time down in the bunks being sick.

Of course, we were down in the bowels of the ship – where you could get the lowest fares – but now and then we could get to the surface. They had some swings on a deck upstairs. I can remember swinging and I think we swung over the side of the ship. For me at 5 years of age here I was looking way down into the ocean – that kinda scared me. We were all sick but those of us who could would go up and get food and bring it back to the others who couldn't get up.

We got ship's fare but, being Hungarian, we no doubt brought some food along. When the Hungarians emigrated they always took a lot of food with them. Whatever they could get through Customs they would use or present to the host here in Canada. I think the Customs people were

5

looking out especially for them, picking out the things they liked and letting them keep the rest! Whenever the Customs people thought they would like to take something home with them, they would say, "Oh, you can't take this because of the rules and regulations." I have a feeling there was a lot of that.

Estevan

We came by rail to the west. The next staging place was Winnipeg. I remember we were stopped there in a holding area. There were a few new adventures. I remember those three-tier beds and us kids climbing up into them. I remember, too, having bread with butter on it, and it was very different to what we'd ever had – it had salt in it! I loved that. We never had salt in the old country.

Then, finally, Estevan. I don't remember getting off the train or Dad being there to meet us. I don't remember much about getting there but the accommodation we went into was the worst I'd ever seen in my short life. My mother was just heart-broken. From the beautiful place they had had in Matramindszent we went into this place. There was a nice view out over the Souris Valley – if you wanted a view – but the house was awful. Just lumber siding and tarpaper. You could see the sunshine through the cracks. We got there in summer but come winter it was bitterly cold. Mother found it very hard.

Dad built us a second house. He got lumber and it cost him $1800. Friends helped him build it, of course. And he sold it in 1935 for $450. Joe and Jim went to Valley View School which was probably only several blocks from this second house.

My older sister was born in the old house exactly a year after we arrived in Estevan. My second sister was born a year later in the same house. (We were all born at home.) Neither the old nor the new house had plumbing or water. We three boys carried water in two tin tubs with handles on each end and two pails from a standpipe two blocks away. This was for drinking, cooking, washing and Saturday baths.

Dad had dug a well about thirty feet deep, by hand, but it dried up shortly. It was useless. There was no rain so we had to haul every drop of water. Mother had the two baby girls and us three boys fighting and horsing around to look after. Dad was away, of course, looking for work, so he wasn't around to do any reprimanding. There was no money. There were other Hungarians there living under similar conditions. I remember in this four-room shack there were always people who needed a bed or whatever. There would be people sleeping in what was the living room/dining room space, and we three boys in another room – we always had other people sleeping there, too. We shared everything, including bedbugs which may have arrived in the suitcases of our visitors. And I can remember the yearly ritual of burning sulphur to fumigate our house.

It was touch and go. Dad lost his job when they shut down the pottery plant. So he only worked October through February in the coal mines. They were mining lignite, which is so perishable. As the summer came along it would disintegrate, of course, so there was no mining job then.

I remember Dad telling us how they were mining in shallow seams. He had to lie on his back and chop the coal just a foot or two over his head. And the water leaked from overhead on him. He would sometimes work two shifts because we needed the money and I remember him coming home and getting washed, then lying down on the floor and groaning in agony with the pain in his legs. They gave them

7

heavy rubber suits at one point but you can imagine how hot it was working in those. We lived some six miles from the mines, so he walked to work and back, of course, each day. Later, he would get a ride in a vehicle without any heat.

We spoke only Hungarian at home. Dad could make himself understood in English, having been over here before us but we kids picked up the English language with no difficulty, it seemed. Yes, I remember the prejudice and the cruelty of the English children calling us "bohunks" and, of course, "highass". Eventually, we asked Dad if we could change our name, as any name ending in an "s" seemed to bring on the tormenting. He said "OK," and thus we have become Hajash – as simple as that – to this day. As we got older, we three brothers could more than hold our own with any of them, so that problem was solved. There were a lot of fights! You bet. We were tough.

We had lots of kids to play with as we were too young to work. But there were no sports facilities. A couple of kids named Szabo (which translates in Hungarian to "tailor") lived across the street from us and we played with them. We didn't have a radio or newspapers, but my friend's Dad got the Sunday Chicago Tribune (I think it was called the Sunday Edition) and the Sports section was huge. I read it from cover to cover, especially anything to do with track and field events. And I loved the American football section with diagrams and illustrated plays and pictures of guys catching the ball. It was the start of my great interest in sports. The 1936 Olympics was about to happen, and I read all about that, too. I played a little baseball with my brothers but I was the youngest so I was always the catcher – where I wouldn't make too many errors.

One of the local service clubs held a yearly field day for the kids. They had races for all age categories. I ran in them all and came home with $1.15 – an amazing sum which I gave to my Mom. And I remember being pretty excited when she gave me back 15 cents.

I remember coming home with my brothers from school playing a game where you called out "cups" or "knives" or "dishes". This was because we had to set the table when we got home and so whatever was called out was our part of the chore. "Cups" was the best call because we seldom needed them. No milk.

Mom and Dad didn't speak English very well, but we kids had no trouble. The "old folks" weren't out in society. The only time they went to town was for groceries so they just pointed at what they wanted.

The seniors, newcomers from Hungary or other visitors, loved to play jokes on the kids. I remember I was pining and complaining about how I'd like to go back to Hungary, mostly, I guess, because I saw my Mom crying a lot. One day, a couple of the fellows said, "We'll help you get a passport and you can sign up and get your train ticket and off you'll go". I remember they took me into some kind of a large building where they went to the counter, got a form and wrote something on it and then said "You sign here". So I did and they said this would start me on my way home. When I got home I told everybody that I would be going home soon. As it turned out I'd signed a liquor order form in the liquor store where they were buying their booze.

These people would tell us stories, and we listened by the hour. Some fairy tales and some made up, no doubt, but we loved it all.

Dad worked at anything he could get. The pay was a dollar a day. We had a garden around the house but there was no water and we couldn't grow anything. But down by the river there were market gardens and Dad got to know the people and for a bit of work he was able to get a little patch of land to grow stuff on.

You were allowed to make beer for your own purposes and could drink cheap beer that way. Well, of course, other people wouldn't have their own facilities for making beer or didn't know how to make it, so they were out looking to find cheaper beer than was available in the pubs or hotels. There was an obvious demand so Dad started making beer for sale. I know we all helped. You could make 96 bottles in a big ten-gallon crock so that's what we began doing in our dirt-floor cellar downstairs. You put the ingredients in the big crock. That's all I know. (I haven't made it myself.) I was only eight years old but I helped with the bottling. When the brew was ready, several of us went down there with our little rubber hoses and our (hopefully) clean bottles. As I said, we would get 96 bottles out of that ten-gallon crock and as long as Dad didn't drink too many of them, we could make, say, $9.60 out of that batch at 10 cents a bottle. We used regular 16-ounce bottles.

Well, this went along fine – fellows came to the house, sat there and enjoyed themselves in our little wee house that Dad had built – with the rest of the family there. They'd be in the living room cum dining room cum bedroom – the "everything room" – and have a good time. This went on for, I don't know, a year or so but, as with all things, something went wrong. The police got wind of these things. People weren't going into bars as they used to and the barkeepers were heard complaining. So the police sent some undercover guys around to pick up people like us. We were raided by the police. One guy was in there drinking beer he'd bought from us so that ended that. Dad went to court, of course, and was put away for a month in Regina where the nearest jail was. In that one month, out of all the time we spent in Estevan, we were helped out by the community and government sources so we had free food for that one month. I was young enough so that it didn't bother me. I didn't feel like a criminal and I didn't think Dad felt like a criminal. He was just trying to keep us alive.

I remember, years later – about 1954 – when I went back to work in Regina for 2 years, Dad came to visit us from the farm in Brooks. I took him out and drove him around Regina. He didn't recognize much. It had changed a lot since 1934, but he showed me all the trees he'd helped plant. That was one of the jobs they did from jail. He was quite proud of the trees he'd planted around the government buildings and elsewhere.

But things got so tough by about 1935 that Dad had had enough so he and Joe, who was fifteen then, hopped a freight in Estevan in January and made it to Brooks, Alberta. Dad had no doubt heard there might be work there. Imagine – how did they keep from freezing? Food? They shared whatever there was with each other as always. Sometimes the rail people would invite them into the caboose. That's how they got to Brooks.

Figure 2: Estevan, the family in borrowed clothing.

Chapter 2 – Life on the Farm

Mickey's family moved to the Brooks area in southern Alberta in 1935 where they settled down to a farming life. Mickey helped with the farm work and attended elementary and secondary school there before leaving for university in Edmonton in 1943.

Duchess, Alberta

Dad and Joe scouted around Brooks, walking to the farms and looking for work. Dad had himself and two sons to offer. He eventually found a farmer – name of Trimmer – near the town of Duchess, north of Brooks about eight miles who needed some help because he had a fair-sized irrigation farm. He grew a lot of potatoes and was into some of the market stuff. He had two boys but needed extra help.

So Dad signed a contract with him and then hopped the freight again and went back to Estevan, sold the house and any furniture – there wasn't much. (Dad and Joe did that trip on the freights three times.) Then Mom and the two babies and Jim and I got to ride in a passenger train. Dad and Joe rode the freight to save the fare.

Dad was hired on a contract that started April 1 for seven months for $100 a month for himself, Joe, Jim, Mother (the lady had an invalid son) and me in the summer months. They got all of us for the $100 per month. They gave us some milk, some eggs, a little patch for our own garden. There was a house on the farm right near their house, so Mom, with the two little girls to take care of, could go over to work for the farmer's wife as well as look after us. The house we had there was a whole lot better than our first house in Estevan, that's for sure. They were good people, from the States, and they treated us well.

I either walked or rode a horse to school. That's another story. One day Mr. Trimmer said, "Here, take the horse", so we put a saddle on and I had a lunch bucket strapped on. This was tomato time, so I had a knife in my lunch bucket to cut the tomatoes with. We were trotting along when somebody jumped out from the side of the road and startled the horse. In turn, the knife started rattling in the tin lunch bucket which scared the horse even more, so he took off, not for the school but at a right angle. I pulled on the reins, but he just kept going. We got off the road, across into the ditch, and there was a little path along the fence. We galloped along there and all of a sudden there was a cow! Just standing there. And the horse leapt over the darn thing! Finally, he got so tired he had to stop. So I got off and led him all the way back to school!

When I got home, of course, I told them what had happened. The poor horse's mouth was a mess – the bit had been broken before and they had welded the darn thing and it had come apart. Anyway, after that I walked to school.

The family worked per the contract for the seven months and must have saved several hundred dollars. Then we got another contract to share-crop a half section for another American who had bought a full section just east of Brooks. He wanted somebody to work the land while he could come up and use it as a sort of hunting preserve.

With the money we saved from the sale in Estevan and the seven-month contract with the Trimmers we were able to buy a couple of horses, an old wagon, some other equipment, – all old – and eventually started to work the land with the horses. We had somebody come in to plough.

14

When we first got there, for some reason we'd settled in a house midway along the whole section – I don't remember why, because there was a house down in the south section where we were going to farm. There was also a big bungalow that the owner wanted to keep for himself. The first winter we were in that first house – the one that was half-way along the section. It was literally across the road from a school – the Sutherland school. This was in the area called the Sutherland colony after the Duke of Sutherland who owned about twelve sections. He had brought out settlers from Scotland, and maybe a few from England, to work the land for him. He had a manager who was supposed to live in the middle house while the bigger one was to be kept for the Duke to live in when he came to visit. Well, he came once. Later, the manager, who had a big family, moved into the "the bungalow" as it was known.

During the first winter in that house, we had to go to the Brooks school as the Sutherland school was shut down. The school in Brooks was four miles away and since there were a few kids around they arranged to haul us all into town in an old car, an old "Model A". I spent grades six and seven in that school and then in my eighth grade, the Duke of Sutherland school, which was right on the property, was re-opened so I went to school there.

In the spring of 1935, when we started farming in Duchess, about ten miles north of Brooks, both Joe and Jim were hired out full time so their schooling came to a close. They worked from before dawn to dusk. Jim was thirteen and a half and Joe fifteen – no more schooling for them. We were all healthy. (In Estevan I had appendicitis and had to go to hospital. I was the only guy that got to go to a hospital! I don't know how I got there, but I remember I was hungry the whole time. So, of course, I wasn't supposed to eat

15

much and they served tomato soup. With that and the anaesthetic, I still don't like tomato soup!)

We tried to grow and raise everything we needed. We had chickens, turkeys, geese, hogs, cattle. We had some grain crops and every kind of vegetable. For meat we would slaughter a hog – usually with a .22 – then stick it, and save the blood (needed for various meats), take that away, then lay down clean straw around the carcass and set it on fire. That would burn off the bristles – most of them. Then you had a big barrel of boiling water nearby and a couple of you would put him in that and then scrape off whatever bristles might still be there. Then put it on the table and take out the intestines, both large and small. Cleaning them was Mom's and my job. The small intestine was awful because you had to get the fat off and then rinse it inside, back and forth, and get all the yucky stuff out and clean it up really well.

The large intestine was used in making a special kind of "pudding". It was stuffed with rice and pork and "other stuff", then it was boiled, and later on fried before eating it. It was really good. When you fried it, it crackled – a special mix of meat and rice. Naturally, it was eaten with bread (as most meat was).

We also made sausage. To stuff a sausage you had to hold this piston up on your stomach. (This may have caused my aneurism!) The piston had a spout set on the end of it and you threaded the small intestine onto this piston. Then one person would hold the end and the guy with the piston had to stuff the meat into it, hold it against his stomach and force the meat into the intestine as it was slowly released off the end of the piston. The other guy had a needle and released any air that might be in the casing, so finally the stuffing moved along and you tied the end off. So whenever the piston was empty you filled it up and kept going. It takes tremendous pressure to get the meat to go into that casing. The guy with the pin can make things easier, but if he doesn't put enough holes in you really have to push! Then you boiled the sausage and then smoked it. We built a little smoke house for smoking sausage, hams, etc. We used Manitoba maple chips for flavouring.

The remaining meat was cut up, boiled, and put into two-quart "Red Cliff" jars. For any leftovers (nothing was thrown out) you had to clean every darn pot you could find in the house and fill all these pots and pans with this meat with the jellied substance on it. And then you had to eat this stuff first. It was OK, but mind you, when you looked at this crud, it didn't look so good. Anyway, that's the way we looked after the meat.

Now for the sauerkraut. It was very important in our lives. Late in the year after a lot of the work was done, it was time to do the cabbage. So we would take the wagon out to the cabbage patch and pick the cabbage. It often had ice on it. We'd fill the wagon, bring the cabbage in, clean it off a bit. Then the two older boys would shave the cabbage on the shredders and Dad would bring the shredded cabbage and put it into the barrel. Then I was put in the barrel, too. Of course, I'd washed several times and had on clean clothes. I would be in the barrel and Mom would come along with a ladle and bucket out the water. I stomped, and Dad would keep throwing in the shredded cabbage, salt, cloves and pepper along with it, and you'd keep going until it got so deep. They'd then put a row of whole cabbage in. Then stomp, stomp, stomp until we put in another layer of whole cabbage, so there were a lot of whole cabbages in there besides sauerkraut. That cabbage was used for stuffed cabbage (cabbage rolls). If we used it properly, the last of the cabbage would be used up by about the time the new summer cabbage was ready. It would last right through until June.

I was put into the barrel because I was the youngest and the other guys were supposed to be doing heavier work. I got to do this kind of work – like cleaning the intestines, and so did Mom. These were jobs for a woman and the youngest boy. She also did the chicken (for meat and soup) at least once a week.

We had a basement under the house and that was where we put the sauerkraut. But it wouldn't keep the meat so it had to be eaten as soon as possible.

We had all kinds of vegetables. I loved kohlrabi and this would be stored in sand. We grew lots of potatoes. Eventually we had 55 acres of potatoes. We ate lots of soup, used some of the meat for that, and wonderful fresh vegetables right out of the garden. Really good. We ate well – seven or eight thousand calories a day, I'd say. We needed to because we worked hard. We'd be up at five and work through till dark.

I didn't do much studying. I attended classes, but after that it was back to work on the farm. Here was my routine: Five o'clock up and get on the horse, go a mile or so across the creek to get the horses (they were usually at the far end of the damn field), drive them back and into the barn, chase them in quickly. Jim would take care of the horses, Joe the tractor. Then I'd turn around and go out and get the cows. They were slow, of course, but I would get them into the barn, put the horse away, then milk the cows – six of them, more or less. Then I'd separate, put the cream in the right place, get the skim milk and feed the calves. You had to teach the calves how to drink. I still have these marks on my hands. My fingers would be raw because they'd suck on them – they had lower teeth – and they'd chew away on your fingers.

That was my routine and when I finished that I had to slop the hogs, then, after that, rush into the house, have a quick wash, change clothes, have something to eat and walk or run three miles to school.

In the summer I would have to go out into the garden with Mom to work. It was a huge garden, there was always work to be done there, and when that was done, out I would go to get the cows. Mom was always busy with something, so after supper we'd have to do the dishes. Dad was a real taskmaster. He wouldn't let us out to play or anything like that. Maybe on the odd Sunday afternoon we'd get an hour off to play.

On the farm in Brooks, I remember I was working a darn old second-hand buck rake, it's called – used for alfalfa haying and such. You fill it and you trip it, but this dang thing was so old it didn't want to trip and I tore the big muscle off the front of my right leg. There was no way I could go to hospital, so it was left, and sort of reattached. That's the way it's been the rest of my life. I can still feel it. It seems it has come "unattached" again – it hurts and has been affecting my golf swing!

At the farm we had visitors all the time – free room and board of course. This is what you did: feed 'em, put them up, and get them started. These were people from our homeland mostly. We didn't have any money, but that's what you did – you helped each other.

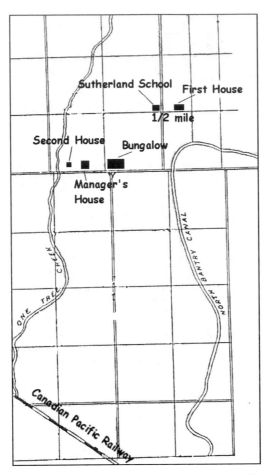

Figure 3: The Sutherland Settlement area north of Brooks.

I'd like to say a few things about the amenities – or lack thereof – on the farms we lived on. First, our living accommodation. We had very few amenities in that small 4-room "crofter's" house near the Duke of Sutherland school we lived in that first winter – 1935 or '36. We had to get the water from town, there was no electricity, we used coal oil lanterns and wood and coal for heating and cooking. At first, we got water from town but then, I remember Dad and the boys had to dig and build a cistern of brick and cement so it would hold water, and then when the water was turned on in the irrigation ditch it was let into the cistern, filtered through sand and that was our supply. In the fall you made sure you filled it to the top, as the irrigation water would be turned off in October. It was not turned on until April or May so you had to make your supply do.

The next spring we moved to a similar house down on the south side of the property. These small four-room houses were duplicates of the crofters' houses that the Scots lived in when they were farming the laird's property in Scotland. These were the kinds of people the Duke brought out, and he built these houses every quarter section or so for them to live in while they farmed his lands. The stove was the only heat in the house. We lived in that house for about four years, then in the bigger, two-storey house. Again, there was no water, no electricity and an outside john, of course, same lighting with lamps. Outside in the barn at night we used coal oil lanterns. We lived in that house until I went to university in 1943.

Basically the heating in our four- or seven- room houses was the cook stove (wood or coal-fuelled), with a water reservoir on the side that held several gallons. For the smoke outlet there was an as-long-as-it-took stove pipe, black, about eight inches in diameter connected to the stove. This long unsightly conduit served as an assist in the heating of the house. It was suspended from the ceiling by guy wires. These pipes, being near the ceiling weren't very efficient, as the hot air tended to stay near the ceiling. Doors had to be left open to allow air to circulate, so the bedrooms got some heat and the rest of the house very little. Altogether, we stayed in seven houses with this type of heating – two in Estevan, one in Duchess and four in Brooks. Even the "mansion"(the bungalow) had stovepipes in the kitchen. Every spring there would be a major cleaning of the pipes, sometimes painting. What a job. What a mess. Reassembling this complex array of pipe and wire was a tedious, dirty job. People today don't realize the problems faced in the old days just to survive.

Figure 4: The "Bungalow" in winter.

Other spring jobs included taking down storm windows and putting up screens. There were lots of flies around, especially in the rural areas. Raising new plants in the house for our huge garden required an early start (February) with careful planning, then moving them to the hot house and then the cold frame so they would be ready by the 24th of May – unless frost persisted. You could say we had a miniature "garden centre" indoors.

The floors in our houses were always cold, so we made a big old handloom, and using leftover rags or patches of whatever we had, we would weave these scraps into rough kinds of mats which we would lay across the floors.

In 1944 or '45 the family finally moved into the bungalow that was by then not being occupied by the landlord, Mr. Taylor – a gentleman from Seattle. He sold us the land as he had promised, and he sold it for just about what he had paid for it in 1935.

As you know, at that time the prices were very depressed and we're talking about $7350 for 750 acres of land, a lot of it irrigated. My brothers and Dad bought the same acreage for $8350, including the three houses – the bungalow included – and that was a large house.

When the Duke sold his holdings, the Irrigation District took over all of his acreage but then they didn't want to be a landlord as such. They offered it for sale and Mr. Taylor had bought that section plus a few acres that could not be irrigated just east of it next to the canal. We had a canal to the east of our acreage and the acreage just adjacent to the canal was pretty badly alkali-ridden. It couldn't be farmed. So we got to farm the south half of that section (320 acres). Of course, the drainage canal or creek was part of it and it took out 37 acres. Across the creek, the land could not be irrigated at that time. On the half section under irrigation there was a slough in a good part of it and that took out a large area as well, so out of the 320, I'd say we were probably lucky to have 180 workable acres or something like that.

About irrigation: This area – some seven thousand acres – isn't all irrigated. There's always land that's too low, alkaline, or too high. It has canals to move the water and then there are drainage ditches. For instance, that section that we finally bought and were farming has a huge drainage creek called the "One Tree Creek" going through it and it uses up about 30 acres in the section of land. It comes from the south and west and goes more or less north through the west part of the section. When I went out to get the horses in the pasture on the other side I would have to wade them across the creek and I'd have to keep out of the waves they made so I wouldn't get soaking wet.

By stressing the seepage and the alkali encroachment from the irrigation canals I may have maligned the project which was the real catalyst for the change of the dry prairie around Brooks to the fertile farmland that it is now.

In the early 20th century the CPR agreed to a grand irrigation scheme including a dam on the Bow river at Bassano, large canals to and from a huge manmade lake (Lake Newell) and a grandiose viaduct (largest since Roman times), 3.2 kms long, up to 20 meters high, built of concrete with an inverted siphon to go under the CPR line (about 4 kms south of the Bungalow.) This complex series of dam, canals, lake and aqueduct did succeed in changing the bare arid prairie into an agricultural paradise (although slowly at first and not during the years of the Great Depression).

The aqueduct, although it provided a real boon to the area, did not perform as had been hoped. The water through-put was not up to expectation and poor workmanship and problems with early 20th century concrete and engineering practises (no testing of materials and design, pressure to complete on a tight schedule). The aqueduct was abandoned in 1979 and an earth canal was constructed alongside. This large earth fill water carrier must be one of the largest in the world and carries 50 per cent more water than the concrete aqueduct could.

Bob White, whom I knew in Brooks and at the University of Alberta, was the engineer for and later manager of the Eastern Irrigation District and can be credited with the immense upgrade of the irrigation system. The Aqueduct is still standing with an interpretive centre nearby to tell of its past glory (and lifeline for people like our family) in the early days.

One of the incidents I remember was when I was about eleven or so, raking hay or weeds into long rows and, if there was really bad stuff in that, we burned it when it was dry enough. So they said to me, "OK, boy, away you go." Off I went with a pitchfork and matches and started burning at one end, heading in the direction of the slough. But just then a big wind came up and it pushed the fire right along the rows and there was no way I could stop it. It just ran right on into the slough. There were probably about 30 acres in that slough – reeds and stuff. Well, of course, that caused a big to-do as that's where the ducks hung out. They had to fly off, of course, and there were some very anxious moments and we didn't know what the full consequences would be. I didn't get a lickin' but I sure learned a lot about fire from that experience.

As it happened the slough came back to life, better than before, so I guess every once in a while it is a good thing to burn things down and start again. But it was a frightening experience.

I remember another time later in the winter when a big storm came up – howling winds and, of course, the animals were out feeding. We had to get dressed as warmly as we could and try to get the cows in as they weren't as hardy as the horses who could weather a storm pretty well. By the time we found the cows and got them back into the barn it was obvious they were partly frozen – the two hind teats were frozen. Come milking time a day or two later the frozen parts were sore and scabbing but they had to be milked or they'd dry up. They complained like hell, of course, and kicked and carried on. To keep kicking down to a minimum you forced your head between the hind leg and body, and this would prevent the cow from using that leg to kick with. Most of the time! I remember our hands were raw and bloody for a week or two. In that storm the ranchers and farmers around lost a lot of livestock. Cows especially. Sheep losses, too. They drifted with the wind and were pushed towards the sloughs where the ice wasn't thick enough to hold them so they drowned or froze. It was a poor time for the farmers and ranchers.

About rabbits. We used to have a lot of haystacks on the property. We grew alfalfa and the third cutting of alfalfa would be real nice and tender. It would stand about a foot and a half high before frost came so we would cut it and stack it. Come winter time, when the snow covered the prairies, the rabbits would come in and attack these haystacks. The preferred one, of course, was the third cutting and they would eat so much of it that the stacks would topple over. People would prop them up; then again they'd topple over. So we said, "Well, enough of this." We had .22's and we'd shoot the rabbits and, of course, they'd stand with their ears up so you'd shoot some more. Then they would run a bit and stand up so you just kept on shooting them. It was really the only way to solve that problem. Of course, we'd skin the rabbits and get ten cents a hide.

We had lots of muskrats, too. They lived in the slough which was in the middle of the property and there was a ditch that went through one side of the slough and they would tunnel right through the ditch, letting water get into the slough. So that was a problem. We would trap them (it was permitted) and skin them and get maybe fifty cents a hide for them.

There was lots of produce. I was the "gardener". We grew everything, as I have said – great quantities of corn and cucumbers and tomatoes. We had so much you could hardly give it away. The corn, I remember, I used to take into town to the Chinese restaurants – there were two of them. I'd get seven cents a dozen – about half a cent for a cob of corn. Not much money but it was something.

We grew many acres of potatoes – Netted Gems. I remember hauling them in to the rail cars in 106 lb. sacks – the extra six pounds for the dirt that was still on them. We got six dollars a ton for them – less than a third of a cent a pound delivered in sacks into the car at the railhead. That was how the farmer made his living.

We also grew seed peas seeding in rows and by broadcast and then we grew the green peas for canning. They were both fairly labour-intensive – you had to keep the weeds down or try to. In the row crop you had to cultivate. I can remember in the very early stages we did this by hand. It was like the old sugar beet business where you hoe it and thin it and it was all very labour-intensive. The broadcast part of it is a lot easier than the row part. Weather was a very important part of the pea-growing business, especially in the harvesting. You had to wait until the peas were ripe and then you cut the roots so as to be able to pick them off the ground. But when you mowed them you had to be careful because, if they were too dry, the peas would pop and you'd lose all the seed. So it was delicate timing. (I remember Dad getting up at four in the morning and the fellows coming in to help with the harvesting. Each of them got a tot of vanilla to start the day. It was a ritual).

We also grew popping corn. This was different from the other corn we grew. It had smaller cobs and produced pointed, sharp kernels. In the winter we would rub these cobs together and then bag the kernels. We would then put a handful of the kernels in a wire basket with some mesh over it and shake it over the fire. When it popped we'd dump it into bowls and put butter on it. This we would eat as a treat while we played the occasional game of cards.

I didn't get a lot of criticism or chastising from my Dad or Mom but my brothers took care of that part of things. If I strayed off the straight and narrow they'd let me know about it. For example, when I was selling produce out of the garden in the town of Brooks, getting our meagre few cents, I'd bring the money home and give it to Mom. But once in a while I'd keep out a dime or a quarter and put it in a little stash. Well, one of my brothers found it and, boy, did he give me hell – so that finished that part of my career!

Despite all the outside work we had to do on the farm, we had to help Mom, especially in the evening – washing dishes and what have you. Once I snuck off to bed, I remember, and, boy, I was hauled out of bed and back to the kitchen to finish what I was supposed to do. So those are the ways I learned.

Again, helping Mom. I remember she had to do all the clothes washing for a couple of babies and all the rest of us as well, including any boarders or friends staying with us. The washing was all done by hand. Mom made the soap from hog fat and lye. It was very crude and harsh. At first, just a tin washboard and rubbing back and forth. Eventually, we got the deluxe model, a glass board, but it was still a lot of hard work. Finally, a year or two on, we got one of those big old wooden tubs sitting up on a stand and with a crank. You cranked and the paddle inside moved back and forth. A tub full of clothes was darn hard work. So that was my job – to do that part of the washing for Mom. It helped build muscles, especially in one arm.

Getting the most out of what we had required some ingenuity. We bought flour by the 100 pound sack (usually Robin Hood). Our basic staple was bread. My Mom would save the sacks until she had enough (usually six), wash them until she got the logo out then sew them together and they became bed sheets, pillow cases and table cloths. The smaller pieces were used for wash rags and foot wraps – sox cost money – so for the hard-wearing jobs like irrigation we would wrap our feet with these sack wraps and when we entered the house we'd take them off and go barefooted. Keeping the family in clothes was a major problem. Mom sewed for herself and the girls, repaired and patched for Dad and us boys. I wore patches over patches. Everything was handed down from older brother to younger. Skates went the same way. Starting from a "used" or "otherwise obtained" pair they would be used twice more by the younger ones. I was fifteen before I got my own pair of skates. Our family was not what you'd call "well dressed" but we survived.

Of course, when we first started, we didn't have any equipment. We didn't have power, horses, tractor or what have you, so it was tough sledding. We hired some tractor work – heavy stuff work – but we had to start buying horses, usually old nags or unbroken horses which my brother would break in for harness work. That's how it went from year to year, steadily getting more equipment, more power, finally getting a tractor.

Then the north half became available. For some reason the fellow doing the north half whom we'd known before – another Hungarian immigrant – left. By then Mr. Taylor was quite happy with how we were operating the south part, and he let us take over the whole section. So we branched out into that. Of course, that kept Dad and the two boys and myself and Mom busy. In addition to growing wheat, oats, barley, rye, flax we also grew soya beans. And then we got into the potato business and that takes a lot of manpower, especially the picking part. Most of it you can handle with a few people, but with picking you've got to bring in a crew, which we did. This went on from 1942 on. We got sick of dealing with potatoes because it was a really dicey crop. Potatoes can have diseases like ring rot which is god-awful.

You're restricted from selling the stuff, so your whole year is shot. Or frost in the fall – there's a delicate balance. You want a little frost to freeze the tops to make it easier to dig. But if you get heavy frost or if you get a lot of rain right about then you're digging potatoes out of the muck. This is another hopeless task, so out of about ten years we probably lost two or more crops. And as I said earlier, I think, we used to sell potatoes, especially in the early part of the game, for $6.00 a ton. It wasn't a real money-maker so they finally got out of potatoes. We used to sell, say, at least a carload in the fall because we had too much for the root cellar. The rest would be put in the cellar and sold during the winter when the prices were a little better.

We didn't go to church. We didn't have time. I know that in Estevan, Joe and Jim sometimes went and Mom went all the time. But nobody on the farm in Brooks went to church until much later. Joe and his wife went to church but later on. (He was still on "the farm".)

I took my lunch to school, usually a piece of bread and jam. I didn't take any meat – it was not the thing to do. You didn't want to sit there eating a hunk of meat with people watching.

I loved to run. When we had recess – fifteen minutes or so – I'd get out and run. Right after school, I'd run home.

Brooks

After grades eight and nine in Sutherland school, I went to Brooks high school. Because of the work needed on the farm, I didn't have time to study. I made passable grades but, when I got to university, I didn't know how to study. I completed grade twelve in Brooks. One particular teacher there, Mr. Albert Fia, helped me a lot. He was a young teacher and was also the sports coach. He taught and encouraged me, and coached me in the finer points of the various sports we played. This was mostly track and field but basketball as well. We didn't have enough players for a hockey team or even a basketball team so Mr. Fia played on our teams, which was agreeable to surrounding teams facing the same problem. He eventually joined the Army, but even then found a way to come to important track and field events to encourage me. He's responsible for getting me into track and field culminating in my becoming, at age seventeen, the top junior track athlete at the provincial meet in Calgary in 1941. I entered eight events and came away with three firsts, three seconds and two thirds. In achieving a vault of ten feet six inches I set a new junior pole vault record. I did reach eleven feet six inches later but not in an acknowledged track meet.

In training for the Calgary 1941 meet (I was out of school and on the farm for six weeks) with no daylight time for training, I would run in the dark. I had entered the hurdle event – I had never hurdled before. To practice I put a lantern at each end of a hurdle I had built from two vertical sticks and a crosspiece, and I jumped over this hurdle over and over again. This was a 120-yard course. I won the event.

I haven't said very much about the two girls. They were growing up, born in 1930 and 1931, so back in the '40s and on they were a big help to Mom. They worked in the kitchen, cleaning, washing and cooking. We used to have a lot of labourers, one or two pretty well year-round, and a whole bunch in potato digging time and threshing time. All had to be fed.

Figure 5: Mickey, Mr. Fia, and Ross McKay

Chapter 3 – University

In 1943 Mickey left the farm at Brooks and went up to Edmonton to attend the University of Alberta where he enrolled in a Bachelor of Mining Engineering program. At university Mickey became heavily involved in sports activities, especially football. Summers were spent working for Imperial Oil on seismic exploration crews. He graduated in 1947.

University

I remember that much earlier I said that Jim and Joe had not progressed very far in their schooling. They were pulled out of school after many interruptions, such as coming to Canada from Hungary – one at thirteen and the other at fifteen. I remember Joe saying that he got up to grade nine. When we moved from Estevan to Duchess, the two boys became full-time labourers on the Trimmer's farm. From then on they were full-time labourers and farmers for their lifetimes. And I should say about that decision, I don't think either boy grumbled or revolted or left home or said anything. I think they were quite willing and ready to do what Dad had put them into. As far as I know, there was no resentment and I knew them pretty well.

So I was the only one who progressed past high school. I had worked with Dad on the farm the last year – summer and winter full time and all through that time, of course, my brothers and Mom and Dad knew that I was trying to go to university in Oklahoma. In the end, this didn't work out but I was going through all the motions and paper work trying to get there.

I didn't especially want to go to that university, but a few of the more influential people in Brooks thought that would be

33

a good place for me. They consisted of the Ingram brothers who ran the general store , Mr. Chet de LaVerne , the local lawyer, Mr. Wes Crook, station agent – all who knew our family – as well as the Carter seismic crew from the States. And our landlord, Mr. Taylor, who got my visa to enter the United States after a seven months' delay. Apparently immigrants were registered on a quota system, and of course, the war years made this all the more relevant. I think it was the seismic crew that got me a scholarship at the University of Oklahoma to study petroleum engineering. It was because of them that I wanted to be an oil man of some kind. They were geophysicists exploring for oil so that was what I was going to be.

The petroleum engineering course in Oklahoma was one of the best in the States. Oklahoma was more or less the center of the oil business then before it shifted to Texas. The family knew I was trying for this but entry into the States was difficult, especially with war time approaching and me from Hungary. The Americans had a strict quota system for immigrants. Consequently, we decided I should go to the University of Alberta to take a degree that would be as close to the oil business as possible. That meant taking as much geology as one could.

By then everybody was pretty well committed to my going to school and to supplying the money – because I certainly didn't have any. There weren't any scholarships and there were no student loans floating around as there are now, either. Anyway, there was no negative feeling about it at all. Nobody ever mentioned that maybe I should not go to school but stay on the farm. And I think the other two boys were enough to satisfy the farming requirements. So I had no qualms about going to university. I don't think my family had any ill feelings about this. As a matter of fact, when I was going to school the first year, they supplied everything – which amounted to about $800. I'd send my clothes home for my mother to wash – the few clothes I had. She'd wash them and send them back, so they helped me in other ways besides the money .

I decided, however, to take Engineering at the University of Alberta. There wasn't a course in geophysics around but I thought the nearest to it would be geology in the mining engineering course with some physics also. That's when and where I got set on course to be a geophysicist and an oil man.

I don't remember how I got up to university in Edmonton but with my paper suitcase, one suit, one pair of pants and just the shoes I had on, a couple of shirts, etc., off I went. I had heard that the DU fraternity house was looking for boarders. This was wartime and enrolment at universities was low. I found out where it was and knocked on the door of Rutherford House (named after Dr. Rutherford, the first premier of Alberta). This had been his house.

I knocked and a fellow came to the door. I said, "I understand you are looking for boarders," and he said, "YEAH!" and hauled me in. And there I was for four years. It was one of the best things that ever happened to me because the four years there were just fantastic. I made a lot of good friends and I got a lot of help from the brothers, especially the seniors. Going through all I was going through, they were really a big help – especially trying to make us study, explaining how to make presentations and such and, of course, taking me along to the many sporting events. Registration wasn't too difficult as the mining course was fairly well set and I guess I let them know I wanted to take that course. So that went quite easily but, of course, how do you pay for it all?

I didn't have a bank account – I didn't know about these things – but somehow I got the money for the tuition fee – $200. That was the main thing. And, of course, there was the room and board. I think it was something like $60 a month for seven months. Then books besides, and a bit of spending money. So I think it was about $800 a year my university cost me – in total, about $3200 for the four years. That first year my Dad and my brothers had to supply the money, but I don't think I felt I was cheating them because I had worked that year and a half on the farm. So things were quite OK that way.

I registered, began to get to know my friends and then the next thing was to get out and check into the extramural activities and that wasn't too difficult with the help of the fraternity brothers. I got involved in track and field and in football. I had never played football before but I had read and dreamt about it and I was ready and eager to go. I did what they told me to do although we didn't have any coaches then – just some of the senior guys telling us how it was done – but I really enjoyed it. Here I was, finally playing a game that I had imagined for years and years. They stuck me on the end, not because I was a good pass catcher but because I could run and hit and tackle – in a fashion. That's where I played that first year.

I remember some of the things that happened that year on the playing field. I didn't get any touchdowns or catch a lot of passes but I did do a lot of tackling. And I remember playing against the Meds because they were there for six years and they were always tough. One half-back of theirs was really good but I could catch him and tackle him from behind. Of course, being over-eager, I got knocked down a lot. I remember once I was flat on my back and some guy stepped between my arm and my body. I flexed my arm and whisssssssssssss, down he went. He looked around to see what had happened. It just shows you what you can do, even when you are down!

I really enjoyed that game. Track and field was OK, but football was the main sport. I didn't have much time after football but I turned out for the Engineers' track and field team and we won the overall competition. The pole-vault was my main event.

I haven't said much about studies but I attended lectures. The frat house was only three minutes from the lecture hall and it was no problem to get there. Sometimes I had a small problem staying awake, mind you, and I wasn't too good at studying. My high school years and the work on the farm weren't conducive to developing good study habits and I had a problem with my courses that first year. Of course, there was always the threat that you'd flunk out of school and away you'd go into the Army. I managed to just barely get through that first year.

At Christmas time we got a couple of weeks off so it was back home to Brooks. I would take the train down to Calgary and then on to Brooks. Of course, it would be winter time. By then we'd been in the potato business for some time and had a big root cellar in the middle of the farm area. It was a covered pit 30 by 120 feet and about 15 feet high. A huge thing. My two weeks were spent out there every day sorting and bagging potatoes. We'd cull and bag them and then haul them down to the rail yard. I seldom saw daylight for those two weeks. First there were chores and then out I would go to the root cellar which was dark except for the lanterns. Those were my Christmas holidays for three years. The odd time in the evenings we'd get to Brooks and see a few friends but not very often.

After the first year was over, it was get out and try to earn what you could to pay for next year's university. I had talked to the Imperial Oil people and told them I would like to work on their crews in the summer. These people would be brought up from the States. (Imperial Oil was part of Standard Oil of New Jersey.) They'd come up to Canada for the summer, then go back for the winter. After the last exam I went to an Army camp in Calgary. It was a two-week camp and we had regular Army training. At the University we had to choose Army, Navy or Air Force to do military duty. I chose the Army (I tried the Air Force but with the Commonwealth training camps here in Canada they weren't recruiting locally) and after school in April we went to camp for a couple of weeks. After the camp I'd start with the seismic crew with Imperial Oil. I looked up friends living in east Calgary and boarded with them. In the mornings I'd go down to the headquarters garage and we would head out to the field with the dynamite truck, the instrument truck, and operating truck. I would assist the operator – laying out cable, digging to bury the geophones. I would keep doing this until we were ready to shoot.

At times I would be well ahead of the recording truck, maybe half a mile, and when I got the OK I would have to run back as fast as I could and pick up the geophones and the cable and move them forward. I did this for the whole summer out in the Turner Valley area southwest of Calgary. We did some refraction work which is a slightly different technique and usually requires larger dynamite charges. Sometimes it could go over 100 pounds whereas the usual could be 5, 10, 20 pounds.

I also worked on the instrument truck and the guy in charge of that was usually a graduate geophysicist or engineer or electrician. The first year it was Frank Spragins. I had known him in Brooks in 1941 and he was a wonderful man. As was his assistant. Both were really great to work for.

We'd stop for lunch, but usually I was so hungry the sandwiches would be all gone. There wasn't much left by noon. By the time I got in at night I'd be starving! During that first year doing this, I wanted to carry on with football. Calgary had a junior football league and three teams – West End, North Hill, and East End. I had a friend in Imperial who knew the North Hill gang – he lived up there – and he talked me into playing with them even though I was living in the east end. In the evenings when we got into town I'd hustle out to the high school in North Hill. I would practice most nights with them and then on Friday nights, we'd play against the other teams at Mcwata Stadium. It was a lot of fun.

And there, for some reason, they let me carry the ball! I hadn't carried the ball in university even though I was fast enough and big enough (around 185 pounds). And here I got to carry the ball and that was really a lot of fun. This went on all summer and we had a really good time.

I remember one or two guys on the team. Bill Gadsby got to be an all-star NHL hockey player. If we were having trouble with anyone on the opposing team they'd say, "Leave him to Gadsby." And he took care of them alright. As a matter of fact, it got so that if one guy saw Gadsby was after him, he'd throw the ball away. It was a lot of fun and we were at the top of the league at the end of my time there. There was another player besides me from university but when we went back to University of Alberta they said, "Nope, you can't go back and play junior football in Calgary." They wanted us to play for the university.

I forgot to say that my salary was now a hundred dollars a month and then they gave us sixty dollars a month subsistence so I think I could save about a hundred and fifteen dollars a month. I think I saved about $460 towards university costs. I couldn't pay all the year's cost but I did pay that much. In addition, I knew that the time I spent with the Company in the summer would be credited to my pension later on, so that was a bonus.

So back to Edmonton and DU house to get reacquainted with the gang again. I registered for second year mining engineering. The first two years were pretty much the same – just a few courses different. So, back we go and into the old routine – new friends and a lot of freshmen coming in this second year as some of the vets were coming back. The first year there were about 2200 students and by the second it had gone up to close to 4000. And back into the track and field. In football we did have a regular senior team and intercollegiate games. I went out to make the team. We didn't have many students who wanted to come out and play football. There were never more than twenty-four of us and a few would drop out and you'd get down to nineteen or twenty players. When someone would get hurt, we would be short of players. In the four years I played – three years senior – I might have missed ten minutes of playing time. Of course, we went both ways, so I was on the field all the time, it seemed. Once I remember running into someone dead on and my neck seemed to crunch up and I was dazed for a while. That was the only time I really felt it. It was tough work but I really enjoyed it.

Then, one day, I said to the coach, "When I was in Calgary, they let me carry the ball. Maybe I could do that here?" So after a while one of the coaches said, "OK," and I got to carry the ball! I was the fullback for the Bears for most of those three years. That was really fun. I loved blocking, so

40

even if I didn't carry the ball, it was all fine and dandy with me. We had some good halfbacks, too. It was great, running and knocking guys down and if you could knock two people down that was better still. A lot of fun all the way through.

I was still having problems digging in to studying and I think I might have missed one or two exams, so that was hanging over me the second summer.

I got into the second summer of work – summer of 1945 – and again it was on the seismic crew. It was getting close to the end of the war but not quite. We still had to go to Army camp and it was at Army camp that I think peace was declared. That was a joyous time.

From there we just stayed in Calgary and I started work on this seismic crew again. Water tanks were needed drilling the shot holes. They needed drivers to find and bring the water to the shot point and help the driller – in general, to be a handy man. That part was quite easy but the difficult part was the trucks. The water trucks were in terrible shape. They brought them up from the States and by the time they got here they were pretty much a wreck. I remember their steering radius was terrible and their brakes were almost nil. So you had to drive in some hazardous conditions with no brakes. I remember very early, soon after I started, when I got into this one loaded vehicle. I was driving down the road and knew where I had to turn in to get to the shot hole location. I slowed it down to where I was going to make my turn but the thing wouldn't turn as it should have, so I took the gatepost out. I had to go and tell the farmer that I'd taken down his post but told him we would fix it, and carried on from there. We had one Imperial Oil man who was more or less following us and taking care of all the problems and complaints that the farmers and landowners would have after the drillers and regular crew had been there.

One other tricky part was the brakes when going to get the water. Where you went mostly to get water was out of a creek. So creeks are in low areas, some well below the level of the land around there, so you had to get this truck down to within a few feet of the creek. Well, the way you did it, you stopped at a spot near the creek, shut the truck down, and looked at the likely spot you were going to back it down to. So you'd find that spot and then find a whole bunch of rocks – big rocks – and pile them on the water's edge and then back to the truck, turn it around, back it up to the edge of the hill and shut off the motor. It would just clunk, clunk, clunk to finally stop, hopefully on the rocks. And then you'd start the motor up, fill your tanks full and then hope you'd get out of there with a full load.

Sometimes I got to do a bit of drilling, especially if the driller got tired. I remember one driller had just got married so he was really tired in the morning. He would let me drill a fair amount while he snoozed in the truck despite the racket.

Other than that it was just long hours – twelve-hour days. And I think it was that summer that we decided to put in two twelve-hour shifts so as to get more holes which the crew needed. So the first time when we went from one shift to two, we worked steadily for thirty hours – drilling and so on. That was quite a start to the new system. We got over that and from then on it was just twelve hours but, when travel time was added on, it meant fourteen hours a day. I think I've mentioned that the pay was eighty cents an hour. Working long hours, that worked out to $9.60 a day for a 12-hour shift.

That kept me busy during the day. I had played junior football the first year but this year I was too old for junior so I went out to play fastball with the Purity 99 team. They had been the best team in Alberta for a while and I'd heard about them on the farm. We'd played a little fastball on the farm. I went out to their practice and, lo and behold, it wasn't fastball they were playing. It was baseball. So now here I was playing baseball which I hadn't played except as a little kid in Estevan when I was eight or nine or so. Anyway, I tried out and they said I should come on back so I kept coming back and finally I made the team and spent the whole summer playing with Purity 99. We had a pretty good team. We played in the commercial league, meaning most of it was Armed Forces – Air Force, Navy and Army. We had a good league going and we met a lot of interesting players. Some of our players were hockey players and I remember one was Pat Egan. He was a hockey player – New York Millionaires (in whatever league that was) – and he was a great athlete, about five feet ten and around 250 pounds. And I remember his neck coming out from his shirt, a huge, huge neck   strong! His face was pock-marked; he was one tough-looking dude and his character matched his looks. For instance, the first time he hit a home run he hit the first baseman, then he hit the second baseman, and then the third baseman and when he came home across the base the umpire just thumbed him out of the game. Just mean. I remember I was in center field and he was left field and the manager let it be known, "If Hajash can get the ball, let him have it." I remember one time there was a drive between us and no time to holler for it. I saw him at the last minute and moved one way and he stepped on me, just below the knee – with his cleats on, of course. And I think if I hadn't moved, I'd have been buried right there in center field. Incidentally, I caught the ball.

And I remember the Olmsteds. Bert was our third baseman and Dean was our pitcher. Tall Dean – he threw a mean ball. We had some good guys – semi-pros who would wander around Western Canada playing for various teams. I have a picture that shows a pretty good bunch of kids from Alberta. We were provincial champs next year. So that kept me busy – working fourteen hours and playing ball after that. We played in Buffalo Stadium which was right in Calgary – Fifth or Sixth Street West, just near the river. It was a small stadium. I remember I could throw a ball from pretty well anywhere in the field and one-hop it to the catcher.

I remember the Army team had three Bentleys with it: Max and Doug and Reg who was the pitcher. He wasn't very good – even I could hit him. I should be careful because they might get after me, but Max and Doug were really good. That Army team was great.

We're still talking about the second summer at university – working on the water truck, etc., and the long hours, trying to save money. Every summer I tried to save as much as I could from what they gave us, which wasn't very much, to help pay for my university costs. With the hard work you need food – a lot of food. So at the boarding house I'd have breakfast and then take a packed lunch which was generally gone in the first four hours and, if I didn't buy anything, I'd be starving. Which I usually was. We came in from shift and I wanted to go to practice, so there wasn't much time to eat. And I couldn't afford it, anyway. I remember every summer I'd be starving! Consequently, I was very thin. I had to wait until I got back to the DU house and then the food was fantastic – and lots of it. I'd go back to school at 180 pounds, even with all the muscles I was supposed to have, and build up to 195 pretty quickly.

I remember that the second year I'd goofed off a bit with all the athletics, and maybe chasing the girls, but I didn't spend much time at that, I know. But there were a lot of things to do – I was president of University of Alberta's track and field club, the Spiked Shoe Club, I remember.

Figure 6: University life was not all hard work.

Back to the studies. I had goofed off, as I said, and had flunked a couple of courses and had to take some exams before the third year, so I let the guys on the crew and the Company fellows know this. They said, "Take some time off and get back and write your exams," and that I did. I took a good week off and tried to bone up. The exams were in Calgary and I wrote them and found out that the good professors had passed me on both of them. By then I guess people knew I was a pretty good athlete, especially as a ball player. And I think this had something to do with the professors and the marks. So I got there for the third year and there were no restrictions after that.

Third year, of course, is regular mining engineering, the engineers splitting into the various courses. I was the lone mining engineer that year – nobody else. Next year, with people back from the services, about five more joined for the fourth year. One of the courses I took was fire assaying. I was very interested in the course and the prof gave me 100. Maybe he just liked my football or something. Nice fella.

By this time I'd turned pretty well to football and there was very little time for track and field. One was always limping around because of one injury or another. We had a pretty good year and, of course, that was the year when Maury Van Vliet became head of the Phys. Ed. department. He was from the University of British Columbia where he'd spent nine years doing the same thing. He was our football coach and basketball coach, and boxing coach. He did all these things. As I found out later, he was a 4-letter man from the University of Oregon and, as you know, that is pretty rare. He lettered in all four: basketball, football, track and field and baseball. He was quite a guy, very energetic, still very young and, as we didn't have very many players, I remember the two coaches joining in on either the offence or defence – wherever needed. They got involved. I remember Maury who was a pretty fast runner (a back at Oregon) going to beat hell down the field with the ball. I finally caught him, dragged him down and fell on his knee. He was limping for several months after that. We had a good year. I was a fullback that year. (Did I break my nose then?) Gosh, I broke it several times. The skin was always rubbed off, probably because of our poor helmets. They'd come down on us and clunk your nose. My nose was raw and oozing – not blood, but whatever oozes out of your nose. Several times the trainers would try to put an artificial skin on it. Well, that didn't work very well and before long it would come off and the stuff would drip down. But my nose was always a problem. It's been broken several times and never reset. In my later years my wife would say, "Why don't you get that nose fixed?" Well, I tried, more than once. But the doctor said, "I think you are getting enough air through there so, unless you want to do it for cosmetic purposes, leave it alone." As he said, the nose operation is no fun. So I never did get it fixed. There was a "king" in North Africa who died on the table getting his nose fixed! Tunisia or somewhere about there.

We played the University of Saskatchewan – local teams – and then BC came into the Western Collegiate Conference. We beat them – twelve to nothing. But the weekend before we were to go to BC for a rematch, we played Saskatchewan. We could always beat them but, in the end, they beat us – physically. They were hard-hitting farmers and they would knock us around. We had too few players – so few substitutes – and our guys were beaten up. I remember limping pretty badly after that encounter. And I pulled a muscle in my left leg – my thigh – and the trainer put ultra-violet light on it to help it. He said, "Let me know if it gets hot." Well, you know you can't feel that, so the consequence was it burned a big hole in my leg. However, we had to practice, so it was rubbed, and the wound kept getting bigger, and finally gangrene set in. We had to fix that up. Anyway, those are the kinds of things that hampered us.

We went to BC on the train and I remember Maury had brought along his five-year-old son, Maury Junior. I remember playing with him on the train. That was in 1945 and, lo and behold, in 2005 he is my neighbour. Living right next door. He's retired now. He took law and geology in university, had a career in both and then went into commercial real estate and is now retired – semi-retired – running a few of his own businesses, selling aviation fuel in remote areas and double-hulled tankers both for storage and moving fuel. A very, very fine gentleman and friend and he is going to be our executor. He, too, was a fantastic football player at university as well as a good basketball player.

I guess I didn't tell you what happened in the two games in BC. After we'd beaten them at University of Alberta, they were ready and waiting for us, and with our limping crew they beat us pretty badly on Wednesday. Then on Saturday they beat us again. So we went home with our tails between our legs. I know Maury, the coach, was very disappointed as it was his first swing back to his old university – to be beaten twice in a row! But those are the lumps you have to take along the way.

During my third summer's work experience we had one day off in Provost – the first of July. A big celebration that day included a lot of sporting events – softball, baseball, some running. Our bunch of guys from Imperial had some pretty good country ball players. We thought we'd enter a fastball team and we did and one of our guys was an organizer, an enjoyable fellow to work with – Jack Cartwright, a geophysicist from the University of Toronto. He originally came from the High River area where his family were ranchers. As a matter of fact, they were ranching next door to the EP ranch. Well, Jack was the ball team manager and he was organizing the batting order for the day. He asked my advice – I'd played a fair amount of softball around and had a little bit of a reputation. We haggled and wondered about the batting order – who's going to be lead off and clean up and all that sort of ball strategy. We sorted out the first four batters and the others after. We were up to bat first and guess what? The first guy up hit a home run, the second guy up hit a home run, as did the third and fourth, so I guess you could say we were batting at 100% on the batting order. Needless to say, we won the ballgame quite handily. I also played on the local team in the baseball tournament and I think we did alright there, too. By then I'd played a year and a half for the Purity team. I played center field for them. I participated in the track events also. It was nice to win a couple of those. One thing I remember: I was being a little cocky, being in the baseball, softball and running events. At the end of the 100 yards I kind of eased up a bit – but a little too early. I was wearing my track spikes which I hadn't worn in quite a while and kinda dug into the ground with them slowing down and went head first. And it so happened that there were some cinders on the track – a country track – and I took a lot of skin off my shoulders. Otherwise I was alright. I played several ballgames after that. It shows you: don't be too smart.

Jack Cartwright – whom I've mentioned – was quite a fellow. Very outgoing and a lot of fun to be around. His family is still ranching next to the EP ranch, though the Prince's family doesn't own the ranch anymore. It belongs to either Jack's family or somebody else got hold of it, but the original Cartwright ranch is still being run by a nephew of Jack's. I am still acquainted with Jack's wife here in Victoria. I get to chat with her once in a while and talk about the old times. She's from that area, too, so she can relate stories about the ranchers and the Prince. One of the stories (I'll try to keep the names out of this) had to do with the reception for Mrs. Simpson. She came out once with the Prince and the local town was really worried about this – what should they do? A lot of the ranching folks in the area weren't loyalists and they especially didn't go for Mrs. Simpson. As a matter of fact, most of the ranching ladies didn't attend the reception ceremonies and had their own little tea party on the side. Of course, the ceremonies included handing flowers to Mrs. Simpson and this gal I know was the flower girl. They weren't sure they should do it but they thought for the good of the town they should and so she handed the flowers to Mrs. Simpson. After that, she and her mother went to the tea party and when they came inside and after the introductions, one of the ladies asked the flower girl to go and wash her hands to make sure she got rid of anything from the ceremony. After she washed her hands she could join the party. So that's how much they thought of Mrs. Simpson. You can delete this or not but I thought it was quite humorous and so does the flower girl who is 80 years old or more now.

There were a number of hazards in being a shooter on the seismic crew. We took it quite lightly but it's a serious job and you have to be careful using dynamite – any size from part of a pound to a hundred or more when doing refraction which we did a little bit of. The shot holes are not all lined – they're just rough holes. This country is rocky with gravel and stone so holes are hard to drill and don't stay open. You run the rods first to test to see if the hole is open or not. Then you put the cap in the dynamite near the bottom and lower it down with your poles and cables. If it gets stuck you have to push on it. You have rods that connect together and most of the time you can wiggle it down. You're holding the wire and the dynamite in one hand and the pole in your other hand and you're wrapped around this thing and wriggling it up and down and trying to get it down. Well, once, I remember, the head shooter and I were trying to plug a flowing well. The way we do this is to put a little charge down just below the surface, a few feet or what you think you can get away with and plug it up and then back off and fire the shot. This usually shuts off the artesian well which is the problem. Then, once, we got the darned thing stuck a little too shallow and we couldn't get it out so the senior shooter said, "Let's fire it," so we did and it kinda blew off the top of the shot hole around there and the darned thing kept flowing and it flowed and flowed. Imperial had to have our shot hole inspector plug it. But it took him a fair amount of time and a fair amount of money to do that.

Another time, I remember, that same summer we were banging away with our poles and cables trying to get the charge down and it wouldn't go down. I said, "Well, I'll see if I can get it up." I didn't want to shoot at that depth so I wiggled it some more. The rods had a little clip on the end and if you could get that down past the dynamite you could pull up on it. I finally got it out but when I pulled the detonator out, the charge had some bumps on it so it was awfully close to doing something that I would never have found out – it could have blown sky high. So it wasn't a cushy job. You had to be careful.

On another case, when we were working this double shift, the early morning shooter would try to load up enough dynamite to last for the day and sometimes this meant throwing it up on top instead of inside the shot truck dynamite container. This one time I'd gone out to take over the second shift and, of course, you take stock of the dynamite which you're responsible for. You had to account for how much was taken out and how much was used. There were fifty pounds missing so we went through it again and again. No, fifty pounds were missing, so we shut down the whole operation. The crew didn't do anything that shift. We backtracked down the road searching both sides, went in to all the farmers or anyone around and asked if they saw this box that looked like the ones we had there. Fifty pounds of dynamite – well, we never found it. We alerted the Mounties, of course, but they couldn't locate it either. Some farmer must have picked it up and taken it home and used it for stump blasting – that's what they would use it for.

Well, I think that's about enough for that summer. Back to university – my fourth year and final year of mining.

I was then joined by at least five more miners who had started their course before the war and had gone away and another who was transferred in from another university, so there were six of us there that final year including the son of the head of the mining department, Malcolm Clark. They divided us into two groups for the year and we had one major project and several small ones. Also, we had to write a thesis on our summer's work and that was a bit of a chore because, chronically, engineers are not good report writers. I stewed over mine and I stewed over many reports later on with Imperial Oil. I finally learned a bit doing that. The year went that way. I was busy with this work and then with football and hockey and track although I didn't do much track. It was football pretty well full time. I couldn't attend track meets because I would be playing football.

I remember later in the year worrying a little bit. Am I going to graduate? Getting a job at Imperial depended on graduation. I didn't have to have high marks or come first in the class. All I had to do was graduate and I'd have a job with Imperial. They had gotten to know me over the four years and knew what my work habit was and what my abilities were but, still, I had to graduate to be able to get the job. That was a worry but, luckily, Malcolm Clark was one of our group and he knew what his Dad, the head of the department, was thinking so he'd let us know how we were doing. I know I wasn't so sure of myself. He let me know I should go and see his Dad a little more often. I had very seldom gone in to see his Dad to ask him questions and get acquainted. Dr. Clark didn't know me at all but I took Malcolm's advice and I'm sure it helped me to graduate. I got to know Dr. Clark better and he got to know me. I should say a bit about Dr. Clark. He did a lot of work for the

National Research Council and then a lot on the tar sands. He did most of the early work on the tar sands in the 1930's and early '40s and many of the techniques involved now are based on his work. So he was a well-known person and, as you know, now the tar sands are a big thing. Companies are spending billions of dollars on projects and eventually it will be the number one producer in the world – even more than the Middle East oilfields. They have hundreds of billions of barrels of reserve there and it's just a matter of getting it out and separating the good stuff from all that sand and then getting rid of the sand – which people forget is also a big problem.

I started working for the Company a few days before graduation. The day after the last exam I went with a seismic group working around Edmonton. They were to the north – Morinville, Legal, up that way. I worked several days with that crew until graduation day. The following day off I went to Grande Prairie to start my career.

Figure 7: Imperial Oil Otter at Peace River, 1952.

Chapter 4 – Early Career in Western Canada

Upon graduating from the University of Alberta in the spring of 1947 Mickey immediately began work with Imperial Oil as a gravity meter operator based in Grande Prairie, Alberta. While there he and Donna (Dowzer) were married. Later that year they moved to Edmonton where Mickey continued to do gravity exploration work. In the spring of 1949 they were transferred to Calgary where Mickey was promoted to Seismic Interpreter, working on the Redwater and Golden Spike Fields. While in Calgary he played professional football with the Calgary Stampeders. In 1951 he was transferred again, this time to Peace River where he continued to work as a Seismic Interpreter and where he played hockey and baseball. In 1953 he was made Chief Seismic Interpreter in the Regina office where he was involved in the discovery of several oil fields on the Alida-Nottingham Trend. Another promotion in October, 1955, took him back to Edmonton, this time in the capacity of Interpretation Supervisor working on the Swan Hills and several other fields in the Edmonton area.

Grande Prairie (June 1947-November 1947)

When I went up to Grande Prairie I was flat broke and I borrowed a little from the Company. They were quite amenable to lending me some money until I got my first pay cheque. Guess what my pay cheque was. It was $200 a month and I still have it here (the cheque, not the money). There were an extra few dollars thrown in (I don't know what for) but there it was and tax taken off it.

In Grande Prairie the first job was to be a gravity meter operator. That was something new for me. We had a gravity party of five or six people and a seismic crew in Grande Prairie. I went out with a gravity meter operator and learned the ropes. In two weeks' time I was the gravity meter operator. The surveyors on the crew located the points at which to take the gravity measurements. But they were always slow and didn't have enough stations ahead of me. So I would go ahead and locate the stations and take the readings. They would come along later and run the elevations and the locations on all these stations.

I went through some pretty rough country up there in Grande Prairie and further to the north. There were a lot of hills, a lot of muskeg and bogs, old lumber trails, and I got stuck a couple of times. Even with the Jeep in 4-wheel drive you couldn't get out. I remember going over to a farmer once to get a couple of horses and they had a hell of a time but they got me out of there.

I remember another time in a big old low lake area that had two or three feet of grass on it you couldn't see what the heck you were driving into. I put the Jeep in low gear and set the steering wheel in a certain direction and then walked in front. When I sensed something really soft I'd jump into the Jeep and try to steer around the stuff. The problem was that every now and then the Jeep would hit a bump and go off in the wrong direction and I'd have to try to catch it.

I also packed that meter for quite a while and I know that September and October, when the World Series was on (which is why I remember when this was) I packed this thirty-pound meter on my back. The meter had to be kept warm using power from a battery but the two became too heavy so we had a helper to carry the battery and our lunch. We had a cable from my meter to this fellow with the battery in his pack. I led and he followed. This fellow was an old-timer from that area – an old horseman – but he was stuck on Coca Cola. You didn't buy it in plastic bottles then – it came in heavy glass bottles. He would bring at least half a dozen and lug them along – and I'd sometimes have to lug him along. Those damned bottles of Coke were quite a chore. Sometimes we did the work walking along railway tracks, for instance. You can imagine what walking along railway tracks is like with thirty pounds sitting well back on your back – not like a backpack that hugs your back. The gravity meter was a round cylinder so most of the weight was well back on your back. You also had to make sure that you didn't fall or drop it or the thing, if it didn't break, would go off skew completely. If that happened your day's work would be shot. You'd have to settle it down or open it up and reset it, put it together again, and bring it up to temperature. It had to be a constant temperature, so once you tore it apart you had to put it together and let it settle down and warm up which could take quite a few hours.

I didn't have any incidents like that but, later on, I did a job of setting in base stations for some additional gravity stations. This time I used a panel truck instead of the Jeep with a different suspension system. It was in the fall and I had to cross a creek that had partially frozen. Driving across, the ice would hold for a bit but when you got to the middle of the creek it would break with the weight of the truck and you'd drop down with a bump. I'd go across and take the readings and come back. Back and forth. Well, the readings didn't jibe after going back and forth on this creek. I couldn't get the same gravity interval between two stations. Of course, I knew something was wrong so I had to take the meter apart and try to determine the problem. Something was probably jarring loose so I reset it, put it back together, put it on heat, put it on battery and by next morning, maybe, it would be ready to go. I finally got it set by tightening up the holding screws a couple of times. Those were the tricks of the trade.

We had a baseball team in Grande Prairie, of course, and I played ball again in the various towns around the area. That was our fun. That was about it except for the courting. I got to be the gravity party chief in the latter part of the year and then we had to move from there down to Edmonton.

That happened about the time when my courtship with my future wife was going along well and this was, say, September. I had met Donna while I was at university at Edmonton about two years before that. The relationship didn't click too well and I hadn't seen her in quite a while. She came up there to visit her father who was working for Motor Car Supply – he was the manager there. I met her on the street, said hello and we started dating. And I guess around the end of September she finally said yes so we set the date for November 1st for the wedding. This coincided well with the move to Edmonton. The wedding group was small, consisting of Donna's parents and my parents who came up from Brooks along with my eldest brother, Joe. Donna had two friends she'd known since she was four years old come up from Edmonton. One of them, Marjorie Keddy, was the bridesmaid. Andy Andrekson, my good friend from university, was my best man. And then there was Margaret Weir, a good friend I knew from university but who was also Donna's friend from way back. The reception was held at Donna's folks' house – a very small group – the people I just mentioned plus a few friends from the Company and a couple of townspeople. We spent the first night of our honeymoon at the Donald Hotel (I think that was the name) with the usual pranks from my co-workers. But we got through that night and early the next morning we were on the road to Edmonton. I did gravity work all the way along the road setting base stations with

57

the gravity meter in the vehicle with Donna and me. She sat on the floor with the gravity meter between us. As usual, my right arm was always on the meter to keep it from bouncing out (not around Donna). It took a couple of days to get into Edmonton. I remember one night we stayed in a temperance-type hotel where they didn't allow drinking. Somehow I had a bottle of beer in our luggage and Donna was worried about what would happen if they found me with that bottle of beer.

In High Prairie, where we stopped for the night, I remember we were to get up early to get going on the road and set these stations along the way. We heard a loud knocking at the door and I said, "Oh, my God, is it wake-up time already?" No, it was a bunch of rowdies coming home from a party, doing their thing and rapping on doors, waking people up, being a nuisance. Another nuisance: When we turned on the lights there were bedbugs scurrying on the walls.

Edmonton (November 1947-February 1949)

We got to Edmonton and checked into the Corona Hotel on Jasper Avenue and about 108th Street. We spent a few days there while we looked for accommodations we could afford on my salary of $200 a month. Of course, Donna was from there. She knew people in the west end so we looked around there. Lo and behold, somebody she knew had a room in their basement that we rented for $32.50 a month. It was one room with a tiny little kitchen and a bathroom you could hardly get into. I remember later on when Donna got pregnant she had to sidle into the bathroom with her tummy below the sink level, it was that narrow. We didn't have a fridge, just an icebox. Anyway we managed to survive.

Somewhere along the way in my gravity time in 1948 I was sent down to Tulsa, Oklahoma, to get training in the gravity meter. Aire Van der Lee and I went down there together. The Company put us up in a hotel, the Mayo, but he and I thought, "Gosh, this is ridiculous." We were paying six dollars per day for the room. We just couldn't see us spending the Company's money, six dollars a night, so we left there and went to the Y where I think it cost a dollar a night for each of us. We slept in bunk beds. I'm not sure we had a room to ourselves. Anyway, later on, we thought maybe we could find something better. We found a boarding house and it was something like fifty dollars a month. We weren't going to stay that long so we stayed and hang the expense.

Anyway, while I was away in Tulsa – Donna and I had been married for several months – we learned Donna was pregnant. But she was having problems due to blood type incompatibilities which eventually led to the loss of the fetus. Following that, the medical advice was she wasn't to get pregnant and we wouldn't have any children of our own. We adopted two children later on but at the time we weren't in the mood to do that.

I continued working with the gravity meter. I was supposedly the party chief for this grand crew of about four of us. A couple of surveyors and I ran the gravity stations off to the northeast and east of Edmonton and all over the Redwater field at that time. This was in early '48 at just about the time Redwater was coming in and we ran a lot of stations there and east of there, exploring other possibilities. I remember doing winter work. The routine was: drive along the main road that was open, turn on to other roads (north- south) roads, put chains on because the snow was deep (roads weren't maintained or ploughed), run my stations up as far as I could go on that road, come back down, stop, take the chains off, drive along the highway to the next road off the highway, put the chains on, set the stations on that road, come back again, take the chains off, drive along the highway, stop and put them on again. This went on all day. It was quite a chore lying underneath the vehicle in the snow, putting the chains on and taking them off. I got to be able to do this pretty quickly.

That same winter they asked me to put in a bunch of base stations around Edmonton. I started at the university where there was a base gravity station. This time I did it using airplanes – two-seaters at first but finally I got a four-seater. There would be just the pilot and me and the gravity meter, the gravity base, and the battery. We took off from the old Edmonton airport downtown. We'd fly out to an area where we thought we'd set a base, land in the field, taxi to the corner of the field, get out, take the meter and the battery and the gravity meter base out, set it on the ground, take the reading, and get it back into the plane. (This usually meant going through a ditch full of snow, so we were up to our rear ends in snow all the time.) Then we would take off and head to the next one. It was quite a ritual.

I remember one day it was really windy and bumpy. My head kept hitting the roof of the small plane, banging away, but we kept doing the job and this one time we landed near a small town. After I'd taken the meter out and set it all up the pilot went into a cafe that was nearby. I didn't know what he was doing. We packed everything back in again and took off. As we got up into the air he reached into his leather jacket and pulled out some paper bags. He had seen I was getting greener and greener. Once I got those bags that did it. But I had to describe these stations so that we could have a record of it for future use. I had to keep working at it. I did this from the Edmonton airport for a good two weeks. Then we got a larger plane and another pilot and did some work out to the northeast where we landed on a few lakes with skis.

I remember one place very well. I think it was Wolf Lake northeast of Edmonton. We taxied to the shore, got the stuff out, set up on the shore and took the readings, got the stuff back into the plane and got in. The pilot revved it up and it didn't move. He revved it up as high as he could and it still didn't move. He said, "Oh, oh, we're frozen in." The skis had frozen to the ice. He said, "OK, I've got an axe back here," and jumped out with his axe. I got out too and started chopping the ice from under the skis. Then we got back in again with the same result – he revved it up and it still wouldn't go. I had noticed that there were some First Nations people watching to see what we were doing. I said, "I'll go over and get those guys to give us a push." So I did. I got them to understand what our problem was. Sure, they came and pushed and I pushed. Then, when we got it moving as fast as they could keep up, they fell off. I kept pushing as long as I could keep up, then I jumped on the float and climbed back in. The pilot kept it moving, hopping from the crest of one snow bank to another and then he finally took off. It was dicey.

Another time – the same kind of thing. The pilot landed in a field and I went over and did the usual things – took readings and climbed back. We taxied to one corner of the field to get the maximum runway. We started there and revved it up – there are no brakes on those float planes. They would rev it up high enough to overcome the friction between the skis and the snow before you would start moving. He started his run across this field and we were getting closer and closer to the fence in the far corner but still not going fast enough to get off so, at the last minute, he wheeled it around (no brakes) and said, "Whoops, we have a problem here....I think the way out of this is for you to get out and without your weight I think I can make it. Then I'll land in a field over there. It's bigger than this one

61

and you can walk over there and I'll pick you up." And that's what we did. I got out and he started off again at the corner of the field, revved it up, just skimmed over the fence at the other end, and took off. I tramped over to where he had indicated and he came back down, picked me up and away we went. That was an interesting episode.

Another time I remember at the airport I had a French Canadian pilot who had learned to fly during the war. I don't think he'd spent much time at it. After that he'd done some bush piloting. We started taxiing at the Edmonton airport (with skis). He was moving along pretty well, but all of a sudden there in front of us was the cleared asphalt driveway at right angles to where we were going. "God," I thought, "I wonder what's going to happen here? If he hits the skis on the asphalt we'll slow down all of a sudden and have a problem." But he jerked on the flaps, hopped over the asphalt runway, landed on the other side and kept going. He capped it off by saying, "I've always been able to walk out from every accident I've ever had!" That was good to know.

Another time, we were heading off southwest from Grande Prairie toward Whitecourt and it was starting to snow. The plane was beginning to ice up and the pilot said, "Boy, I've got to get down as low as I can to get out of this stuff and hope it doesn't ice up any more." He got down low but I, being the navigator, of course, couldn't see anything to navigate by – no big lakes or rivers or what have you. He wasn't a good instrument navigator so we were lost. He got up a little higher and started circling around and around until he finally found a beam into Whitecourt, headed in on that and landed there. By then we were getting low on gas so he borrowed some gas and we finally got back to Grande Prairie.

Another trip was to Peace River from Grande Prairie to set a base there. We flew to Peace River and set down on the river there. The Peace River has tremendous banks on it and we set down on the river in the valley right next to the town and taxied over to the bank. I got out to take a reading on the bank but couldn't get one. It wouldn't come on dial. I said, "Oh, oh, we got a problem." I should have reset it differently back in Grande Prairie. We'd come too far north and the gravity was much different than back at Grande Prairie. I said, "Well, I think we've got to head up the high bank of the Peace to see if I can get a reading up there." It was darned cold and here we were – just the two of us. We weren't going to lug this thing up any hill. I think the surface of the Peace River is about 600 feet below the plain where Peace River town is located. Anyway, a guy in an open Model A was coming by and we stopped him and asked him if we could bum a ride up the hill. We had to get a reading with this machine so away we went. He took us up the hill and we'd get part way up and I'd get out to see if I could get it on dial but no, not yet. We had to get up higher, so we went almost to the top where I finally got a reading.. But I guess with the meter being out in the cold, even the battery couldn't keep the temperature even enough. I think it strayed a bit. I didn't realize it at the time but, later on, when we tried to tie in to other stations, it proved to be inaccurate. But, at any rate, it was an exciting event. We, of course, got down and back to the plane and back to Grande Prairie.

That was a different part of my gravity meter adventure. But we did use those stations later on for the gravity work, especially the next summer when we had to do some work in the Pigeon Lake area southwest of Edmonton. We took our crew and set up in a trailer camp that the Company provided for us. We also rented an office in a house. We had a couple of surveyors but we needed another so a new guy was brought in. In those days we let employees use vehicles to go to town. This fellow was new and wanted to explore the area and, of course, the girls. So he took a girl out around the area for a little drive and before he knew it he came to the end of the road. There was no bridge over the creek in front of him and he had driven right in – had wedged the Jeep between the bridge abutments. He walked the girl home and returned to camp. About 1:00 a.m. he knocked on our trailer door, woke me up and said, "I've got a bit of a problem," and he described it. Well, we couldn't do anything about it at one in the morning, so I said, "We'll wait until the morning and then we'll have a look and see what we can do."

In the morning we went out and there it was, wedged in tight as a drum, water washing almost over the roof. So we went to the nearest town and to the garage and described the situation to the tow truck driver. He said, "Oh, sure I'll come out and we'll get it out." So he came out later that day and we hooked his winch equipment to the Jeep. I had to get into the water to do this and I can remember there were all kinds of things in there – leeches and so forth – but I finally got it attached to the back axle. The tow truck driver said, "OK, I'll give it a try." He had it almost out and hanging there, but then he couldn't raise it any higher. He said, "Well, that's no problem – I'll just put it in gear and drive it ahead and then we'll be out." Well, he put it in gear, let out the clutch and the front wheel went backwards and the back wheel came forward! The frame just buckled on his vehicle. So there we were, with the Jeep hanging suspended and this vehicle with the buckled frame unable to do anything. So he had to let the Jeep back into the water and that was the end of that. He had to get somebody to tow him back to town and then, of course, there was the big problem of what do we do now. What about this poor guy? Do we pay him or what do we do? I don't know how it all came out but we had

64

to phone our office in Edmonton and get them to bring out their cherry picker, a huge machine that could lift tons of stuff. They sent out a couple of guys, just backed in there and lifted the thing out like it was nothing. It cost our crew a fair amount of money and I got a lot of flack for it. I tried to take the blame for this guy, but I guess I got hell for letting a new surveyor go scouting roads in a strange area. Later on, I found out his eyes weren't very good.

After that we did spend a few months in pleasant circumstances. Pigeon Lake is a nice big lake where everyone goes in the summer for vacations. I had a good time playing horseshoes with a lot of the local people. Eventually, we finished the job there. All we were doing was spending some money on an acreage that Imperial Oil had there. So it wasn't a big to-do.

Calgary (March 1949-February 1951)
In another phase of my career I was transferred down to Calgary to the Exploration Head Office for Imperial. At that time it was in the old Albertan building, 2nd St. W. and 9th Ave. This was in March or April of 1949 and Donna and I looked for accommodation. We found some out in the Roxboro area just along Elbow Drive, across Mission Bridge and to the right. Again, it was in the basement of somebody's house. It wasn't any specific room, just space in the basement. We just had curtains separating us from the rest of the basement area. Anyway, it was cozy and comfortable and warm.

In Calgary I got into a completely different type of work: geophysical seismic work interpretation of seismic data. This was done in quite a big office. There were at least ten of us geophysicists in one big old "bull pen" as we called it. There were probably just about the same number of young ladies there to assist us. We each had a write-up girl. We called them to do all the early work on the seismic records before we started doing the interpretation of them. But for me it was all new. I had not been exposed to reflection seismic work before. I worked with the very sharp senior interpreters there. I worked on the Redwater field with Wes Rabey. Boy, he could whiz through those records a mile a minute, wheeling through and picking out spots where the critical points were, where the reef went out and where the oil-water might be and so forth. He was a sharp character. I learned a lot from him. Besides that, I had my own crew to follow and two of them I followed one year. I had to learn a lot and it was tough sledding. Some of that early work was pretty tough. The records were hard to correlate and difficult to interpret. In addition to that, I also worked on seismic velocities. These are critical to our work because you have to convert the seismic times that all the reflection seismic work is measured in to depths. The seismic waves travel down into the earth and are reflected and recorded on the receivers (geophones) on the surface. These data have to be converted to depths so velocities are very critical.

In all the wells we and other people drilled they did a velocity survey. You measure the velocity of the rock in the well at a lot of different intervals. These data are recorded and are then available so that when you start relating the depth to the various seismic or geological horizons you can relate them with the velocities that you obtained from the well. I worked on that, calculating the velocities that you obtained from these velocity surveys – mapping them. I would do that one day and another day I would do the interpreting on my own crews. Another couple of days a week I would work with the senior interpreters and give them whatever help I could while also learning from them. It was a very complete schedule and a very interesting one.

66

I spent the time from March 1949 to February of '51 in Calgary – in the bull pen – learning interpretation of reflection seismic data and in understanding velocities of the sedimentary section. It was all very interesting and I really enjoyed it. That was, of course, a full-time job and more than full-time if you wanted it. We spent a good number of hours working on it – just grinding away. There were a lot of data involved, a lot of minute detail, but it was fun and I was gaining knowledge and experience.

But I was still interested in football. The Calgary Stampeders had a football team and early in the year they had spring training. I tried out for the team and they said, "Yes, come on," so I went through their spring training, all of it after work or on weekends. It never interfered with the work.

I would walk to work, of course. I didn't have a car. I would walk the couple of miles to work and a couple of miles home. When it came to football practice, I don't know how I got there. I'd stay at the office long enough and get a quick bite about 5:00 p.m. before I would go out to practice at about 6:00 p.m. We'd go until about 8:30 practicing and then I'd get home somehow – I don't know, bus, walk, or bum a ride four or five miles from where we used to train at Riley Park, back to where we lived in Roxboro. By then I was really beat. Of course, you had to eat because you had to keep your strength up. This went on for the whole year from June right on through November and it was tough going. I wasn't a very heavy person so I was getting back to skin and bone again. And, you know, playing football, you need the weight to bounce the people around. But it was a lot of fun and, of course, much different from playing at university. The game was much faster and much more involved.. But I enjoyed it and we had a good year. Calgary had won the Grey Cup the year before – in 1948 – and in

1949 we won the Western League quite handily. We beat Regina in the two-game total point playoff – not as handily as we'd won the league. We played Montreal in the Grey Cup. And that's a story in itself.

We got beaten there. Here's my version of it. We played at Varsity Stadium in Toronto on a Saturday – I forget what day in November. It had snowed and frozen and when we got out there in the afternoon about 1:00 p.m. it was starting to thaw a bit but that field was like a sheet of ice. With our cleats we were slipping and sliding all over the darned place. Our attack technique was sharp-angled cuts – and pass plays were the same thing – you'd cut, fake and slip. Well, we were slipping all over the place. The Montreal gang were wearing tennis shoes. They were running loops in their running attack and the same thing in their passing patterns. Filchock, who was an old NFL quarterback, just lobbed them – lobbed them to his receivers. Our attack was sharp cuts, fake, getting in the clear – and the quarterback would fire one in there. Well, if it was a little off, the receiver would try to correct and he'd go flat on his back. So, overall, I think that was the big difference between the two game plans. They out-coached us. They were much smarter in their game plan than we were. Despite that it was a close game – 28 to 15. We had one touchdown called back due to one of those crazy things. Linemen weren't supposed to block more than five yards ahead of the line of scrimmage and I guess one of our guys went a little too far. We'd scored a touchdown on the play but it was called back. Anyway, we lost and we were dejected, of course.

We had taken the train down for three days, practiced at Appleby College which was west of Toronto then but now is in Toronto. We stayed at a place called the Pig & Whistle, just west of the College. That was a real dive – a motel. I had to take a week of my vacation to be able to play in that

Grey Cup and days off for the road trips we had during the year. We had to play Saturday and Monday on some weekends. That may be surprising to some people. We played back-to-back games Saturday and Monday and then we'd get back to Calgary by Tuesday. That was the routine. Edmonton had just joined the league and that was the league at that time: Regina, Winnipeg, Edmonton, and Calgary. We could beat Edmonton pretty handily. I think we were unbeaten during the season until the second game of the two-game total point Western final. I think Regina beat us by a point or two in that game. But not in total points. It was a lot of fun and a lot of hard work and finally a disappointing end to it all. I played flanker. At university I had been fullback, but here we had Paul Rowe who had been fullback for years and another young fellow from Vancouver who had played with them the year before so two fullbacks were enough in those days. Anyway, I played flanker and corner back on defence.

We had some interesting characters on our team. We had the two ends, Woody Strode and Sugarfoot Anderson. Well, Woody was a nice guy, and later on he became famous for playing leading roles in movies. I remember "Spartacus". He was the black gladiator playing alongside Kirk Douglas. Dead now. He was a wonderful man, about six foot five, a beautiful build. Wide shoulders trimmed right down to nothing at the waist. The other guy, Sugarfoot Anderson, was something else. He was not a very nice character and I don't think he was a big asset to the team. I'd be behind him on defence and had to work around him to do a lot of my work. He was a showman and he'd back up into my way. The odd time I had to go right through him to make the tackle. Anyway, it was quite a year and for that I got $500. I was pretty tired and beat by the end of the year. Down at the office they let me know I'd better decide what I wanted to be, a football player or a geophysicist. I decided then I'd be a geophysicist, not a football player, so the next year I didn't go out. I watched them but didn't play. The next year they collapsed – not because of me. They brought in a hotshot from down east and forgot that one halfback does not a team make. You have to have a line to spring him loose. I believe Royal Copeland was his name. He'd been a hot shot with Toronto. So the next few years the Calgary Stampeders were a very poor team. They really dropped from 1948-49.

I had more time then to spend with the Company and to learn more that next year – 1950. I kept working with the Redwater gang, working on the velocities and I also had a couple of crews I had to follow up in the north country.

Along the way I've neglected to say anything about the family and some weddings. My middle brother, Jim, married a girl from Drumheller in 1945 while I was still in school. I came from Edmonton to Drumheller and participated in the wedding. I was best man.. We had a great time. Jim and his bride returned to the farm and for a while lived in the bungalow but then moved on to a property across the road where he'd bought a half section.

Then my brother Joe and sister Liz had a big double wedding. It was a real lollapalooza, that one. I don't know how many were invited and how many came that weren't invited. It was held on the farm. The family was living in the bungalow at the time and it was the headquarters. For the entertainment part we had a big garage that we'd built between the crofter house and the seven-room house and they expanded it to double the size. That was where the evening's festivities were – the meal and the dancing that went on after the wedding. I was supposed to be the security man for the whole thing. I'm not in many of the pictures that they took of the wedding party because I was otherwise engaged. When I first arrived, they realized they didn't have enough booze. "Why don't you drive up to Bassano" (which was at that time 40 or 45 miles away) "and get some more booze?" – meaning beer and everything else. So that was my first job.

Then I was security. People would come to the window in the basement of the middle house and say, "Throw up a case of beer," and we'd throw up a case of beer. Of course, some of the people who came to the window hadn't been invited. They were kind of the town bums and we had to watch out for them – there were several around and, of course, a few of them got into fights.

At the end of the evening there is usually a bride's dance where, for a certain donation or whatever, you'd get to dance with the bride. That was a way of giving a gift other than a present to the bride. So there were two brides' dances, of course, going on at the same time, one at each end of this big garage. My brother Joe had asked me to be the watcher of his bride's money, so I took care of that part of it.

I don't remember what time of the morning my wife and I retired to the bungalow. I had the money for Joe and his wife on a big platter in front of me so I just wound it up into a ball and shoved it in my pocket. Before I went to bed I shoved this big wad of bills into our cruddy suitcase – just shoved it in there. The next day we got up late in the morning and I realized I'd better get rid of this money. I reached into the bag and pulled out the wad and gave it to my brother, saying "Here's the bride's money." "Thanks," he said. "Good job."

The wedding and its aftermath went on for about two days and Donna and I went back to Edmonton to our little basement. I think it was the first evening we were back that we got a phone call from Brooks from my brother Joe who said, "Brother Mick, you don't happen to have any of that bride's dance money left? We think some money's missing." I said, "My God, I don't know what would have happened to it, but how do you know there's some missing 'cause I just took out the big wad and shoved it in my suitcase." He said, "Mother-in-law put in a $50 bill and she had her mark on it and it wasn't there." I nearly had a heart attack! I said " I'll go through everything in the house here and see if I can find the fifty dollars." Fifty dollars was big money so Donna and I went through everything, everything. Couldn't find it, couldn't find it. Finally, I looked into the darned flap pocket of the suitcase and there stuck inside was the $50 bill that had just peeled off, and stuck there. Boy, was I embarrassed! I 'phoned him right away and told him we found it. I sent it down to him but I'm sure to this day, or until she died, the mother-in-law suspected that slick Mickey was trying to make off with her fifty dollars.

There were a lot of other things about Calgary. I told you about the first house we lived in, in the basement. There were really no amenities but it didn't cost us much. We couldn't afford much, so that was alright. No fridge – we had to do without one. From there, after a few months we moved across the Elbow towards town, just a block short of the Mission Bridge. Just a two-room place – a bedroom and a living room and a small kitchen. No fridge, so again pretty meagre digs. Of course, we had other things to do. We couldn't do much in those small accommodations so I played a little bit of golf with the Company gang – usually the odd outing. There was a municipal club, Shaganappi, up the hill. I played there a few times in the wind. If you had the wind at your back you could hit the ball a long way, but facing into it you had a problem. We played one or two other courses in Calgary as well but we couldn't afford to spend much time or money on golf courses.

There was also softball with the Company gang. We had some good players and some good games. We played a little softball in the summers when I worked on the crews in the field. I remember Jack Armstrong was one of the fellows, a geophysicist on the crew who went on to become president of Imperial Oil.

In Calgary we played against local kids. I remember Bill Gadsby was one. He was a catcher for some of the young teams. He was a good ball player. I remember his catching style. Every ball he caught was backhand. Every ball – even a far inside ball – he'd contort and jump over there and catch it backhanded. That's quite odd for a catcher, but that was his style. I remember Bill – he became all-star in the NHL, a defenceman for Chicago. He was known to have a face with more cuts than anybody else's. I think he had about 300 stitches just in his face. His defence style was leaning forward, head forward, backing up. His head would get the stick or the puck first, thus the many cuts on his face.

In each of the places we went to – from Grande Prairie to Edmonton to Calgary to Peace River – we had our own friends that we worked with in the Company and knew from before. But we also mixed in with the communities and got to know a lot of people and made a lot of good friends. For instance, the first group in Grande Prairie in 1947-48. There were over ten of the gravity or seismic crew personnel who got married to local girls there; that's a major involvement with the community. That went on in every place and we would play with the local ball team and hockey team. And we hired a lot of the local people – young girls to help us as office staff, for example – and some of these people we've been friends with ever since and manage to see now and again.

Peace River (February 1951-May 1953)

In early '51, the Company decided that they would decentralize and open up district offices for us geophysicists and explorationists. So they opened up an office in Peace River and Dawson Creek. I was to be a Peace River man. I went there in February of 1951 and spent a little over two years following seismic crews, mainly doing reflection and a little refraction. We enjoyed those two-plus years. We lived in a new apartment complex – in the basement. We didn't have children and I was more or less the live-in janitor. I took care of the fire and what little else needed doing – not very much – but it was a pretty nice place to stay and not far from the office.

Peace River was a small town of 1,000 people or so at the time, set in the valley of the Peace River and we loved the area. There was lots to do. We curled, bowled and I played hockey and baseball with the town teams so we had lots of fun. We made our own fun, too, and met a lot of good people there. Jerry Rempel was up in that area. I'd known him before and he's been one of my better friends for years. He's still around and we keep in touch with him and his wife, Lois. We met other people there who have become very good buddies over the years. So then in May, 1952, we decided it was time to adopt, so we adopted our daughter, Patricia – sometime in the spring or summer. She was born March 5th. We adopted her when she was a few weeks old and had a lot of fun raising her – a really lively youngster and while we were in Regina we adopted our son, David. He was a few months old at that time, born Dec. 30, 1953. We adopted him when we were in Regina in 1954, but came back to Edmonton because of a complication – you were required to be a resident of the province so we went back to Edmonton and adopted David from there in 1954.

Back to Peace River. I've talked about my work there and told you about our living accommodations. We visited a lot back and forth – lots of parties. We also curled and bowled with our company gang and I played hockey. I remember an incident out in Fahler, I guess it was. They had a lot of French people there. A couple of our young boys got into a fight with some of their guys. I – being a defenseman – went over to make sure everything was fought fair and square. They weren't beating up on our young guys, so I just stood around. I saw a lady standing by the boards where the fighting was going on.

She had a big purse in her hand and was whacking one of our guys over the head. So I went over and said to the lady, "Don't hit him – let them fight." But, oh no, she kept beating away. So I went over again and gently gave her a shove backwards and left. The fight ended. After the period was over we went back to the dressing room and while we were sitting there, there came a big bang, bang on the door. A guy burst in and said, "Where's the guy that pushed my wife and knocked her over? She's in the hospital now giving birth to a baby!" Apparently, the gal was nine months pregnant but, of course, I didn't realize that. Anyway, nobody said a word and finally the guy cooled off and left and that was the end of that one.

Regina (May 1953-October 1955)
We bought a new house for $10,000. No landscaping of any kind, no garage, just a little place – I think it was 960 square feet – and guess what: We didn't have enough furniture to fill it. The dining area was completely blank – nothing in it. It was tough sledding trying to make the payments. By then we had an old Chevy car and tried to keep it going.

The geophysical work was just a lot of fun. I was the senior interpreter and my chief geophysicist gave me lots of room to do my own stuff. I got involved in some new kinds of work. I had been about six years by now in the geophysical business. Almost the first two years were, of course, gravity. I'd learned enough that I could do some things – good interpretation. We worked closely with geologists. That was the one big plus that Imperial had in that they realized you had to have geologists and geophysicists working together. Jim Wood was the fellow I was working with at the time. He was from England and he was sharp, well-spoken and a fine gentleman. I learned a lot from him and he helped me understand the geology of the area I was working in. With that I managed to find several oilfields for Imperial Oil on a play called the MC3 Trend in the Mississippian subcrop area in the Estevan Oxbow area and into Manitoba.

We drilled and made a discovery there, Alida #1, in 1954. A little later we drilled Nottingham and then, later, some others in the same area. It was all freehold acreage and you had to wait until you had most of the acreage on the anomaly before you drilled. So you didn't just find an anomaly and drill it. You had to find an anomaly and make sure you had enough acreage on it to make it worthwhile and then drill the well.

Later on we got enough acreage on some of the several anomalies that I had pinpointed and several oilfields were developed in that area.

We were in Regina two years and work took up most of it. Working on the new house took a lot of time and effort. I had to put in the lawn, both front and back. The plot was pure prairie and the sod was tight. I had the back ploughed up, I remember, and each furrow was one long solid piece of sod. Before getting ready to put lawn in, I let it sit for a few months, at least one winter and spring, and then I went with my shovel and broke down each furrow – about eighty feet long in the back and just whammed, whammed, whammed, trying to break this furrow up into smaller pieces of sod. A friend of mine said he could borrow a truck. He was a horsy type, and he knew a place where he could get horse manure. So we loaded up horse manure and brought it in and spread it over the back and let it sit for another year. Finally I could break up the sod and cultivate it and put some grass in. And I finally got the grass to grow. I think we even used some local human stuff from the Regina sewage department. It would be mixed in with the soil – just put a little bit of it in to spread on your sod.

That was Regina and, as I said, we made friends there. We had two really good friends who lived across the street from us, the Hilliards – Buzz and Jean. They're still alive and well. We haven't seen them lately, but we do communicate and find out how they're doing through mutual friends. We did a lot of things together. I remember Buzz was manager of the meat packing plant – Intercontinental Packers downtown. He'd come home for lunch and on his way he'd go by his favourite bakery and bring us home a loaf of fresh bread. I used to come home at that time so I saw him every day at lunch time.

Buzz's boss, Mr. Mandel, used to visit him once a month. Buzz would buy a bottle of Mr. Mandel's favourite Scotch. After they had their go at the bottle and Mr. Mandel had gone back to Saskatoon, Buzz would invite me over to finish the bottle. (A true friend.)

Buzz and I used to go golfing about three times a year out at Boggy Creek. That was a public course and it was very cheap. I also remember playing at the Regina Golf Course which was next to the RCMP training barracks, and we'd see the horses and riders training. Then, when we were transferred in the fall of 1955, we had to leave our good friends behind.

We bought a new house and had to paint it (using oil-based paint – horrible stuff) and I remember when we first moved in we had a flood in the basement. The odd thing about housing in Regina is that most of the city is built on an old lake bed and the water did curious things to the soil. Whenever it rained, water soaked into the first few feet and it would expand and that expansion would push upward on the substructure. The pillars would push up on the ground floor and your furnace, which was usually down there on the basement floor, would be pushed up and, of course, something had to give. The give was the cracks in the house and the walls, especially around the doorways and the furnace which would bow in. To alleviate this, people would drill or dig a sump in the basement and bail the water out of there and pour it into the drain or, if you put an automatic pump in, it would come on once the water started coming up into the sump. You'd also take out the regular pillars holding up the floor of the house and put in jacks that you could screw up and down. Then you would string some wire along the pillars so you could see if any were shifting up or down. So if you saw this wire misbehaving or upstairs in your house you saw the crack being forced upwards – a pressure crack in other words – you would rush down and ease off on the pillars. Then in the fall when things dried out to ease the pressure down below, your cracks would go the other way and you'd go down and crank up your pillars to keep the floor from sagging. So it required eternal vigilance to keep your house on an even keel. Everybody knew that this was the problem in Regina. So when you sold a house, people would see these cracks and you'd just say, "Well, that's the way it is," and everybody knew that. It didn't depreciate the house value as it might have.

I'd been out of football for a few years by then (this was Regina 1953-4). I'd finished playing in '49. The regular Stampeder team decided they would have some old-timer games against teams in Regina and Winnipeg. So the Stampeders started getting their team organized. I heard about this in Regina and I contacted them and said, "Hey, I'm down in Regina and you're coming down here. Can I come out and play with you?" They said, "Oh, sure," so on my own I'd go out and race up and down in the area trying to get in shape. I remember the place where I did most of it was in front of the College and Sacred Heart Convent. There was a wooden sidewalk of good length there. I could go to beat heck on it. Running on those boards was a lot easier than on cement or the regular road. But, of course, a few boards were missing so you had to be careful. But, in doing this, I started to get in shape. When the team arrived on game day, I was in good shape – or better than most of them. I played pretty well throughout the whole game. I can remember the last play of the game – an end run coming around right end – the strong end always. I tackled the guy and he fumbled. I recovered the ball and started racing the other way, but the referee blew the whistle to end the game. We beat them quite handily. Keith Spathe, the quarterback for the Stampeders, who had been the quarterback when I'd played with them, had just retired so we had a young good quarterback. And that was one of the big reasons that we won. We went on to Winnipeg and played against them. They couldn't quite field enough of the old-timers so they brought in a few from the Intermediate League. We had to play against some pretty active young fellows. But again, we managed to beat them. No big problem. It was a lot of fun – I really enjoyed it. I was in good enough shape that I didn't feel the pain too badly! Really enjoyable – both the game and then afterwards with the guys.

Well, that was Regina. It was a very good time in my life, those two years in Regina. The interesting technical work and finding the oilfields was something special.

Edmonton (October 1955-May 1960)

We moved to Edmonton in the fall of '55. Donna and the kids went up earlier (her folks were living there at the time) and managed to organize a house on 142nd Street and 107th Avenue. It was a good spot and the price was right at that time, I guess. The house was a little bigger than the last one in Regina. We paid, I think, $12,300 for it.

I was with a new group. Most of the people I knew but there were a lot of younger ones, too. I was the chief interpreter of the group. I had a large organization, about sixteen interpreters under me and I had to plan, organize and evaluate their work and help them, teach them, direct them and still do some of the stuff that I was expected to do as the top geophysicist – like velocity surveys, velocity logs and the final interpretation of geophysics into geology. That's what I did for five and a half years in Edmonton. The first office was south of the river in the university area near the south end of the 109th St. High Level Bridge in the Noble Building. Our house was across the river to the north.

The new job was a little different and, right off the bat, I had to get involved in budgeting and talking about the technical problems that go into budgeting for the next year. I was to be the chief interpreter and we had a lot of geophysicists – I think about sixteen of them. We had a bunch of girls also who helped us with the details so I had quite a crowd to supervise and organize – and then I had my own work in velocities. I was senior man in that and I just carried on my own work in addition to the supervisory and instructional work I did.

Of course, all the prospect names were new to me so it was a real wrench. My counterpart, the senior geologist, had been there for a year or two and he was well acquainted with all these and was ahead of me. I settled in and did what I thought we should be doing and tried to help as much as I could and learn as fast as I could for the budget talks. But the first few years were a little heavy going and all the knowledge I had and the techniques I had learned till then were not that effective yet in any of our plays we had there. But later on I became more effective as a chief interpreter and worked on several interesting plays. The Judy Creek-Swan Hills play happened about that time. Home Oil had made a smart discovery in the middle Devonian reef. It was geophysically a very difficult play. The velocity change of the reef to the off reef was very subtle, especially on the back reef side. Not at all like in the Redwater and Leduc area where it was sudden, from, say, 16,000 to 10-11,000 feet per second. Here it was 16,000 to 15-14 depending on the amount of carbonate in the off reef area. A discovery was made and we had acreage in the area. We had done seismic there and we did a lot more after this initial discovery by Home. We had a good block of acreage from the government. We had to make a relinquishment on this acreage and decide what part of those few sections we were going to keep. I got involved in that with several other interpreters. It was an important play so we put a lot of work into it. We had a big discussion at the end as to what was the best acreage to keep, where the most likely chance of finding the reef edge would be, and where the oil trapped in the reef would be.

That was interesting and a lot of fun and I used my velocity knowledge in this case. We had seismic velocity surveys in wells but, in those days, a lot of them were one-receiver velocity surveys, one-receiver geophones and only a few used two receivers. Because of that, there were some problems getting the proper velocity in the off reef shale as well as in the reef because of the problems with the method. I had previously worked on velocities for years including velocity surveys, mainly one-receiver types and had seen the really technical nitty-gritty problems of single receiver through the shale and the contaminated shale in the bore hole and even in the two-receiver logs where the first receiver wouldn't penetrate as deeply into the sediment and would go mainly through the mud. The second receiver would go further into the bore hole and get a truer measurement of the velocity but the difference between the two didn't come out with the right interval velocities of the shale and the carbonate. But I had my own technique. Pretty well everybody knew the velocity through the carbonate, so I just set that as the norm and the remaining time was due to the truer shale velocity. I think with that I came up with much the better answers. We made a selection based on our consolidated best guess as to the best acreage. I think Imperial got their fair share of the Judy Creek oilfield as a result. It was a very difficult carbonate play. I think that was the biggest play going in those years. We worked in the Mississippian part of the section also, west of Edmonton. It was slightly different than the Mississippian I had been working on in the Regina area and there were not quite the same problems. I tried to transfer the knowledge I'd gained back there into this area but it wasn't quite as applicable. But overall it was a good five and a half years.

The oil business at the time was pretty slow. I can't explain why it was so sluggish. But it was slow and promotion in the ranks was slow. Raises were really slow. Some of the guys, I can remember, went three years before they got a raise doing a normal, average job. Later on, I can say that when I went to England and the Middle East, every year your salary was looked at. If you didn't get something in the year there was something wrong. But here, during those late 1950's, I guess things were really quiet in the oil business in Canada.

Despite the slow pace here there were opportunities overseas. I hadn't really wanted to go abroad before, but I saw that the Iraq Petroleum Company wanted a senior geophysicist to work in Iraq. I don't think there was a salary stated, but it was something very different. I didn't know much about the Middle East oil business but it sounded interesting. I remember applying for the job and then being asked to go to New York to talk to the head of geophysics there in the New York office, Dr. McNatt.

I had to take my shots first and on the plane to New York I shivered and shook all night and didn't sleep very well. I stayed in a hotel, the Abbey, near the RCA building in New York, 6th Ave. at about 52nd St. People in the Company called it the "Shabby Abbey" and it was pretty shabby. Anyway, it was a place to hang your hat. I had my interview with Dr. McNatt and met a few others. Jack Armstrong was there at the time, working in Producing Coordination. He was a senior man in our organization and he'd been the chief geophysicist in Calgary when I was there in 1948-49. He'd also been on that crew in Brooks back in 1941 so I'd known Jack since then. We had a chat and I remember a shoeshine man coming into the office to shine Jack's shoes. I was impressed. Jack asked me about the situation, what was I doing there and why was I applying for this job since I was from his home area and Imperial Oil. I said, "Well, things are just a little slow back there." I told him I thought that, after five and half years in Edmonton, I'd pretty well done my thing and given them all the ideas I had and it was time to do something else, so this was the something else. He didn't say anything more about that, but I think he was worried that there was some problem – a rift or something like that up there. There was none of that. It was just slow, and everybody above me was moving slowly and I thought I was moving slowly after the success I had had in Regina and then five and a half good years in Edmonton.

So the end result was, by late May, I had been advised that I had the job with the Iraq Petroleum Company and we set about organizing ourselves to get over there.

Figure 8: Oil in the desert.

Chapter 5 – Baghdad and the Iraq Petroleum Co.

In June 1960 Mickey was transferred to the Iraq Petroleum Company. He and the family traveled to Baghdad where he took up his new position as Interpretation Supervisor, outlining some major oil fields including Rumaila and training Iraqi geophysicists there until IPC's exploration activity in Iraq came to an end in March, 1962. The rest of the family then went back to Edmonton and Mickey spent a year as Interpretation Supervisor working on IPC acreages in the Trucial Coast (now United Arab Emirates) region of the Arabian (Persian) Gulf.

Baghdad
The first assignment was to be in Baghdad. The amount of information we had in Edmonton about the assignment and the conditions and whatever you should bring were very scanty. Some of the information we got was almost medieval. "Bring your tennis whites" and things that were just as ridiculous. But we did our thing and took our shots. By then we had the two kids. We couldn't take much but the few things we could take we got organized. The idea was to travel light – not to take too many things that would cost too much. We decided to send a few things by air instead of by sea because that would take too long. In early June we got down to New York and shacked up there for a few days in the "Shabby Abbey". It didn't impress my wife but the kids had a good time for a couple of days and then away we went on TWA Airlines. It was a night flight to London and lo and behold who was on that flight but William Bendix. He was a heavy in the movies in those years, and here he

was on the plane. The kids got to sit on his lap and bother him for part of the flight.

We got to London and into the Brown Hotel on Oxford Street just east of Oxford Circus. It was a little old English hotel they put us into and because it was our first hotel in England, we couldn't compare it to anything else. Later on we found it was down near the lower end of the pole. But from there I got to the Iraqi Petroleum Company office in London which was nearby (and of course that's the reason they had put us in the Brown). The IPC office was in an old department store on the northeast corner of Oxford Circus on Oxford Street. I met the geophysicist and got some information about problems I would face and we got to know each other well. I also talked to the personnel people about what we could take and what we could do. Then a couple of days later, off we went on a charter plane to Iraq.

The Iraq Petroleum Company at that time had a charter from London to the Middle East and to Basra which is in the south of Iraq. Our aircraft was an Electra, one of those planes that weren't supposed to fly over 250 miles per hour or they would shake apart. This was what they had decided after a few accidents with it. KLM ran this charter for them. It was a night flight. We got to Baghdad after this slow journey. The service was tremendous, of course – you'd say first class – because it was a chartered flight. We got to Basra midmorning and it was hot by then. This was the early part of June. We'd missed the air connection with another flight from Basra up to Baghdad so we were delayed a good six hours at the airport which we found didn't have air-conditioning. The amenities were sparse. My wife had worn silk stockings on the trip. She sat in the airport with those stockings on and by the time we got on the plane to Baghdad six hours later she was a basket case.

We finally got out of that airport and up to Baghdad. Luckily we were met by a very nice Dutch employee of the Company, Nick Zylstra, a fine gentleman. I worked with him for the seven years I was with IPC. He was a wonderful man. He was waiting for us at the airport, sent there by the Company. He was in charge of the geophysical group. On the way into town he tried to give us as much information as he could. We arrived during a several-day holiday. I'd never seen so many sheep and people as we saw on the way in. Nick had been there for a couple of years and got us into the Baghdad Hotel which was the only air-conditioned hotel in Baghdad at that time. It was quite new. We got in there with the two kids and started to get acclimatized. We met representatives of the Company and got indoctrinated. I can't remember going to the office but we were contacted immediately by Nick, of course, and others later. After a few days we were put into temporary accommodation. One of the employees was away on vacation so they put us into their accommodation for about two weeks.

I remember being in the hotel with the family and having dinner after which we listened to some music. Soon one couple got up and started dancing. We'd just taken some lessons in Edmonton before we left, South American ballroom stuff, so we got up and did our thing or tried to!. We had a good time with just one or two other couples. We didn't realize that my exploration manager was there having his dinner at the same time and I guess he was impressed with these newcomers getting up and dancing in Baghdad in such times. It was just two years after the revolution and people were cautious about showing any merriment.

My exploration manager was a French Swiss and later on I got to know him very well. He was a fantastic man, solid, good to his people and good to us. He, of course, worked in

London but just happened to be out there. I hadn't met him in London so it was in Baghdad we met for the first time.

When we got into our temporary accommodation, it was a real change. The first big thing that hit us was a swarm of cockroaches. This house that we had to stay in for the first couple of weeks had been empty for maybe a week or so. The other people had gone on vacation. When we opened the cupboard or drawer a mob of cockroaches would come out. There were people you called at the office, named the "Estates Office" and we'd phone them, "Get up here, there are cockroaches everywhere!" My wife, of course, was not used to them, so was very upset. The fellows from this office were all local guys and constantly badgered by unhappy tenants, but they'd come out and tame things down a bit, but the roaches were there the full two weeks we were.

I started going to the office with a group who would get together and take a taxi. We were in the southeast part of Baghdad as it was then. We would go right through the middle of town, past the main square in the middle of town and then across the one bridge across the Tigris. The office was on the other side where the parliament building was – but which hadn't been used since the revolution. We'd get together and the taxi would take three or four or five of us to work. Work was from 7 a.m. to 2 p.m. and then the taxi would bring us home. We'd have lunch and a snooze. Then we would head over to the club that we were allowed to join, an old British army club called Alwiyah.

One morning on the way to work going through the main square in town before going over the bridge we saw a horrible sight. On each of the twenty foot high lamp posts was a body, hanging by the neck, put up there during the night by the government to warn the people, to keep them in line, no hanky panky, no revolutions. Those six bodies were there for days before they were taken down. That was the way the revolutionary government tried to keep the people in line. It seemed to work except there were others that kept this in mind – for example, the first revolutionary leader, Kassim, lasted from 1958 until '63, and it was said his own air force bombed his residence and killed him. And after that several other leaders were deposed, most of them due to foul play.

So that was our initiation into Baghdad. I should go back a bit and say what Iraq Petroleum Company was. It was a consortium of several major oil companies. Shell, BP, CFP and Mobil and Esso had one share together so we had eleven and seven-eighths per cent. A five per cent share was kept by a fellow by the name of Gulbenkian who had brokered this concession deal in the Middle East for these companies several years before. Iraq Petroleum Company was operated by a board composed of representatives of these companies plus personnel hired from the U.K. area. They would borrow employees of various expertise from all the companies as needed. The Company had the full concession for all of Iraq – both exploration and production. They also had concessions in Qatar, Abu Dhabi and Dubai. At one time they had concessions in Oman and Dhofar which they had given up before I got there.

Iraq had been a monarchy up to 1958. The British had more or less set up King Faisal. The new government had just built a new parliament building in '58, but the people and some of their armed forces rebelled and said, "Enough of this, we want it to belong to the people, we want our share," and started a revolution. They quartered the prime minister, killed several others in the hierarchy, took over and elected a fearless leader of their own. When we were there he was a fellow named Abdul Karim Kassim. He was a little strange and I'll go into that later. (He wasn't as strange as this last guy, Saddam Hussein, not quite that bad, but it was scary working there. Negotiating with him was apparently nearly impossible.)

After the revolution many of the country Arabs came into Baghdad and set up homes. (There were about 250,000 of them). Most of them plastered their mud abodes against the fences of the established residents anywhere in the city. There they awaited the distribution of the land that had been taken away from the large landowners (mostly Sheiks). The government tried to get them out on to land, but most of them didn't go. Those that did were unsuccessful. Before the revolution they had been mostly labourers for the Sheiks and didn't know how to farm for themselves. They ate the seed grain they'd been given and most drifted back to Baghdad and other larger centres. Iraq had been self-sufficient in agricultural products prior to the revolution but while we were there relied on much imported food. Flour was imported and was full of bugs, and the ladies sifted it through their stockings.

The work there was really interesting. It was so different from what I had done in Canada. The people were different; the country was different. Everything was new and strange but very interesting. I learned the geology of the area and became familiar with all the geophysics that had been done before. I had to do this as quickly as I could. With my thirteen years with Imperial I'd had enough experience to be able to contribute to their exploration program. Of course there were a lot of things I couldn't do because we didn't have the equipment and personnel to do them, but it was fun trying to teach them. I worked on some huge fields while I was there.

We had about six local geophysicists in the office, some very new, and a few senior ones like Nick and my boss –

who was an old geophysicist, not an interpreter. I had a lot to show them and teach them. I also worked over a lot of the areas and some of the fields and that was really enjoyable. And soon after arriving I got to go out and visit all the areas they were working in. In the north, Kirkuk is the big field, then northwest of there is the Mosul area and then I went on further west and south and then far south into the marshes. Down there they were using Cheramie marsh buggies. They had been developed in Louisiana and IPC had a couple of those out there. Besides that they had marsh boats, aircraft propeller-driven speed boats they used to whiz around the canals and other waterways to get through the marshes. We worked in reeds 10-12 feet high. You had to knock them down and tramp over them to plant your geophones and fire your shots in the marsh. It was very interesting.

When we were there, our company was negotiating with the leader and the Iraqi government about relinquishment and further agreements and it was a very tense time. The local citizens had their problems and once in a while they would get riled up.

I remember one situation very early in our stay. As we were asleep in this strange house there was a loud "rat-a-tat-tat" like machine gun fire and then fire and flashes of light out in one direction. We were apprehensive and worried. We looked out the window and saw these lights and people running up and down the block and wondered what was going on. Was this another revolution? I tried to 'phone the office to find out what was happening. The connection with the night watchman there was poor, but I got the sense that nothing much was happening. So we calmed down and went back to bed. I'm not sure I went to work the next day.

When I did finally get to the office (I don't know if it was the next day or the day after), it turned out the Iraqis had opened a big new building of some kind and what we had heard were the fireworks going off late that night. That seemed a dumb thing for the leader to have done because he riled up his own people, too, I'm sure, with all the noise and firing.

Later on we got a kind of grapevine organized and that's how we communicated. If there was something boiling up we would be alerted through the grapevine and told not to come to the office today because to get there we had to take a taxi across the Tigris and if anything happened I'd be over there isolated from my family on the other side.

There were other things. For instance, to go out of Baghdad on a picnic or to visit the surroundings you had to have a permit. You also needed a permit to have a meeting of more than seven people in your house. Things like that were very restrictive but generally we tended to ignore the little things. You had to have a permit to go outside the city because you'd be stopped on the edge of town by three sets of security people. There were two types of police and then a third guy in dirty old ratty clothes who was the security guy. He could read whereas the others guys couldn't and he was the person you had to worry about.

I remember another experience that really bothered my family. A crew was building pipelines in Iraq at the time and we got to know the manager quite well. He invited us over to a reception he was holding for some of our company people – his own people, of course, and some local people. There was a little booze and we were all feeling pretty good – or most of us anyway– and chitchatting back and forth.

Well, as it happened we'd previously been contacted by some people from the government saying, "We're trying to produce a brochure for tourism and we need some pictures of people here at our ruins and would you and your family be in our pictures?" So I checked around with others in the Company and they said, "Sure, go ahead." So I agreed to go. However, I had to arrange my vacation to fit their schedule so there were negotiations back and forth over when was it going to be, and I had to keep adjusting my plans accordingly.

At the time of this reception still nothing had happened so this was on my mind when I met the Minister of Tourism there. I mentioned this business about his group trying to take these pictures of the sights in Iraq which we were going to be involved in and asked him what was going on. "I never heard of it," he said. So we bantered back and forth and he kept saying, "No, I don't know a thing about it. Don't bother me, go away." I'd had a drink or two or three, and I finally said, "Go to hell," and walked off. I didn't realize it, but apparently he was livid, went to the host and said, "Who's that guy and what is he and I want him out of here in twenty-four hours." Our host said, "He's not my concern, he's just a member of the Iraq Petroleum Company working here – I'm sure he didn't mean anything," and so forth. I knew the manager quite well. The Minister wouldn't accept that. He was going to go to higher authorities, meaning Kassim, I imagine. The manager came over to me and said, "You know, you've got a problem here." Of course, I didn't want to cause him any trouble. He had enough trouble of his own. I'll relate a bit of that later. But I worried a bit. I didn't go to the Company and tell them anything about it, but I'm sure the Company found out and it probably went right to the top manager. We had a manager for Iraq – a very nice but tough Englishman whom I knew. I didn't sleep very well for several nights and checked around with my buddies at the office, "Have you heard anything?" "No, no." Finally, I guess it cooled off. I think the end result was that my manager had more stroke than the Minister of Tourism did.

I don't think Tourism rated very high in Iraq and I guess Kassim had other things like lease relinquishment and keeping his people happy instead of worrying about tourism and somebody being slighted. So it passed, but it was a scary time for my family and me.

There were similar incidents that happened along the way. I remember once another Iraqi employee and his family who had a daughter and we with our two kids – we thought we'd like to go on a picnic into the north country and visit the Kirkuk area. We got our permits. I had an old Nash Rambler that had a problem with the radiator. It would overheat and you can imagine overheating in Iraq. Because of this problem I always had an old jerry can full of water in the trunk. On this trip I led the way and this other fellow stayed behind in his car so if I had trouble with the radiator he could help me. Along the way, of course, we were stopped any number of times by the security people and, as I've said, at each one of these security spots there were three sets of police, including the scruffy guy in civilian clothes who could read. When you handed over travel documents to the other guys, which had pictures on them, if they had the page upside down, they'd know to turn it around the other way but they couldn't read anything, including the Arabic.

But we finally got up to the oilfield area. Kirkuk is a surface structure. It's a big oilfield, one of the first oilfields found and developed in Iraq – in the late 1930s. It was still being drilled and developed while we were there. There was a golf course with a club house. In the evening we went up there and we could look down on all the oilfield paraphernalia and you could also see the eternal fires that were mentioned in the Bible.

Figure 9: The "Eternal Fire" near Kirkuk.

These fires were caused by a gas seep that had been burning for centuries. It was right there; you could see it from the golf clubhouse area. We actually went down to it in the evening. A shepherd was there with his sheep and while the sheep were outside the ring he was inside (where it was warm) playing his flute. The fires covered quite a fair-sized area, a quarter acre perhaps, with little fires all over the place. It wasn't just one gas flare like some of them are; there were several that had erupted and were burning. I don't know how the shepherd felt the next morning, but there was a little hydrogen sulphide in that gas and he probably had a headache.

During the Second World War the Company and the officials tried to put out these gas flares in case the German bombers came to bomb the field. They did put them out, but they caught fire again – lightning or something, and they couldn't keep them out. Also during the war the Company plugged all the oil wells and, later on, while I was there,

IPC had to re-drill wells to produce the oil from the field. (I assume that the wells were plugged so that the Germans could not use them in their war effort).

Another interesting thing while we were there, in 1961, the Company drilled a well with a huge drilling string (by then they had a lot of knowledge about the structure and reservoir). They completed this well with an eleven and three quarter-inch casing so that oil came up at the rate of 100,000 barrels a day. They fed it into its own separating plant. They say it was really a tremendous thing. The ground would shake all around the area and there was a tremendous noise because this well was producing so many barrels per day. There are not many, if any, other wells that produced at that level at a steady rate. It's only because the formation is very porous – fractured, faulted – so that the oil just pours in, just like that. I don't think it's producing now because at 100,000 barrels per day, if they kept that up for a long time it would go dry pretty quickly and the oil-water level would come up past where they had perforated.

Speaking of oil-producing capabilities, I should mention the one big field in the south, Rumaila. It borders on the fuzzy boundary with Kuwait. While we were working there, there was a gentleman's agreement that neither the Company working on the north side in Iraq or the one working in Kuwait would drill anywhere near this indistinct border between Iraq and Kuwait. Both would keep more than 5 kilometers away. Well, we did that and they did that. I worked the field and had enough data that I could predict where the oil-water level was – where the contact was. I predicted on my mapping that the structure plunged to the south. The south dome was plunging down to the south at the boundary. The oil-water level in the field met the top of the reservoir right about this border. So there was no likelihood of Kuwait having much of the Rumaila field.

That didn't mean, however, that there wouldn't be an argument over it between the two countries.

Figure 10: "Cheramie" marsh buggy.

Later, probably in 1962, after Kassim had pretty well kicked the IPC out, the oil companies with concessions in Kuwait apparently decided to drill a well near the border and claim their part of whatever was there. So they stuck a well right near this fuzzy border. Of course the Iraqis saw this and figured they had to do something about it. I guess it was Kassim who told his southern army commander to "Get in there and make them tear that down and haul it away." The British on the other side sensed that there would be an incident with that oil well so they stationed five hundred paratroopers in Bahrain. The story is that when the Iraqi southern commander heard how strong a force was there he cabled back to Kassim saying, "I will not." I don't know what happened to that southern army commander or whether this account is even true.

It is the case, however, that when I was there, the Iraqis were known to be poor and unreliable soldiers. The British, when they were there during the '30s and '40s, wouldn't use them for backup of any kind, even in their camps. They just didn't think they were good fighters and they weren't good camp personnel, so the British used others, either Kurds or Assyrians, not Iraqis.

At the end of our first two years in Iraq, as I said before, all the acreage had been taken away from us as of April of 1961. We stayed on and tried to show that we weren't going to be a party to not fulfilling our contract. We carried on for another year, more or less, doing work in the office, finishing our mapping. There's always lots to do in geophysical work – reviewing your data and polishing up your data and, like myself, working on the Rumaila field – working the heck out of it and then working on further new prospects. I had all the other contract personnel come in and help me in that work. But eventually, by March of 1962, they were pretty well gone and whatever company people were there in exploration were either let go or sent to other parts like Qatar and Abu Dhabi.

We were in Iraq somewhat less than two years and it was really exciting. But things happened fast there. For instance, less than a year after we were there, I was already out in the fields visiting the crews down in the marshes. (There were flamingos, thousands of flamingos down there). While I was there the crew got a telegram from Head Office telling them to shut down and bring all the equipment into such and such an area. They looked at me, "What's going on?" and I said, "I don't know what's going on. I didn't hear anything about this when I left the office." This was early April, 1961, less than a year after I got there that orders came out to shut everything down. There was nothing to do but shut down and bring in the equipment. All the crews from the country – we had about 4, I guess – were shut down. All the personnel came and sat in our office in Baghdad. It turned out that the Company was going through negotiations on relinquishment with the government and they couldn't come to an agreement. Our company had a negotiating team

98

headed by a Frenchman and they'd meet with Kassim and say, "Well, I think we can offer this much." So he'd say, "No that's not enough – I want such and such percentage," and they'd come back and agree to this and he'd say, "That's not enough, I want more." This went on until finally it came to the point where he said, "That's it. You're shut down and from now on this is how it's going to be." That's when this April 4th shutdown happened. They just shut us down completely. But the Company's attitude was, "We're going to carry on with our contract commitments as they were. It wasn't us that brought this termination, it was you, it's your fault." So we in the office – interpreters and other geophysicists – kept working our data, new and previously acquired. I did a lot of work that next year, interpreting and directing people in the office, and getting them to do interpretations, which they hadn't done before. We ended up the following March with some real good maps, that, eventually, I guess, the Iraqis got.

But by the end of March the next year the decision was made. We'd played it out and they were not going to relent. All the exploration personnel and a lot of the production people were moved out. The situation was this: Kassim said, "All you're going to have is the producing acreage that you have drilled and producing oil from wells that have been tied into pipelines. That's all the acreage you are going to get." That amounted to about 4% of the total country where we had had 100% before. So, all the exploration people left. A few others and, as I've said, my family packed and returned to Canada.

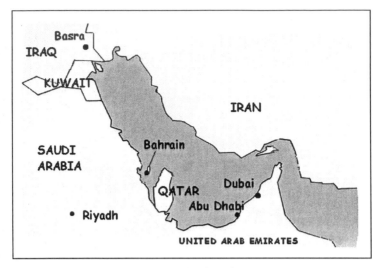

Figure 11: Sketch map of the Gulf region.

Bahrain and Abu Dhabi

My family returned to Edmonton in February, 1962, and I went down to Bahrain to work on the Qatar, Abu Dhabi and Dubai acreage that we had there. In March I set up with a couple of other guys in a little house that we called the "chummery" – three chums running this house in the middle of town. The island of Bahrain itself is just a big geological structure with an oilfield right in the middle of it. The top of the structure is eroded, which happens in many places, and it's a bit low on the crest of the structure and that's where all the facilities are. The town of Awali, I think it's called, is right in there. They even have a golf course down in that area.

Bahrain had been the center of commerce in the area for years but since the 1970's Dubai has been taking over. Bahrain was mainly known for pearls. Just off shore, the locals dive for oysters and bring them up from a great depth. It's a real habitat for pearls.

100

The town of Bahrain itself is on the north end of the island. There's an airport and I think there's now a road connecting it to Saudi Arabia. People come over from there. When you see somebody sitting in a club drinking beer you'd know he had just come from Saudi Arabia because they didn't have beer there. The ex-pats have their own booze which they make in the company towns. I visited there a couple of times and tasted some of their good martinis and Scotch, but they didn't make beer. Liquor was available in Bahrain. They had a quota permit system, just like we had in Alberta. There was a certain amount you could get quite freely. But since quite a few people who didn't drink also got permits you could get their share as well so the supply was pretty well unlimited.

We had no operations in Bahrain. A different company ran that operation. The Bahrain oilfield was one of the first oilfields found in the area. I think they discovered oil in the early '30s. I worked the Qatar, Abu Dhabi and Dubai data from there. I had an office in Bahrain, of course, and then would go from there to Qatar. We had a small geophysical operation. Qatar at that time had an oilfield on the west side of the island and you can see the surface structure there. I visited the field and facilities. We had a small seismic program that I had to help organize. We had a couple of crews in Abu Dhabi so I became familiar with the operations there, too.

Abu Dhabi was especially interesting. I knew a bit of the geology there. They had made a discovery at a place called Murban, not far inland from the main town of Abu Dhabi. I think Abu Dhabi had about 15,000 inhabitants. Most of them lived in the desert and moved from place to place and then would come to the one big town, Abu Dhabi, once in a while. Shakhbut was the Sheikh of Abu Dhabi. He was an old skinflint, unlike the Arabs in Saudi Arabia. He wouldn't spend his money. They were making money from the oil, increasingly so, as you'll find later, but he wouldn't spend it. There were stories of how he had millions of English pounds stashed under his bed and how some of it rotted. Apparently the British authorities replaced it for him. Shakhbut knew his people and he knew his camels – he loved his camels. In fact they say he knew his camels better than he knew his people. His family didn't go along with his way of governing so about a year or two after that they kindly asked him to step down and let his brother [Sheikh Zayed] take over because his brother spent money more easily. That did happen, quite calmly and peacefully in a family sort of way. It was a small, interesting place.

Figure 12: The "pub" at Abu Dhabi.

Oman is on the east coast of the peninsula and there are a whole bunch of other little sheikhdoms between Dubai and Oman now known as the United Arab Emirates. The British were the main influence in the area and had a military force there known as the Trucial Scouts, I think. We met a few of them along the way. There's an interesting oasis, the Bahrami Oasis down between the southeast corner of Dubai and the northeast corner of Saudi Arabia. Oman fringes on the east side of it. They'd been arguing about who had the rights to that oasis. As you know, water rights are a big thing in these desert areas so this was a big issue. When we were there the oasis was more or less under the control of Abu Dhabi but, after I left the area, sometime in 1967, the Saudis and others who were vying for it reached some kind of agreement. I think the agreement was that Abu Dhabi would give Saudi Arabia a 5 km.-wide strip along the south border all the way across from east to west and for that they would maintain the rights to this oasis. These particular oases are better than the typical ones. The water is of a better quality and it's a flow – actually an artesian well – fed from a source in the mountains to the east in Oman. We visited there. You can see the flow of water; it's quite substantial and very important in that area.

Well, as I say, I worked both Abu Dhabi and Dubai. It's fairly flat along the coast. The Gulf waters are quite shallow and later on we did seismic work in this shallow water. It was quite interesting. We'd drill off a barge – shallow holes – and lay geophones in the seabed. We did a survey there. I can remember whenever you got into really shallow water you'd have to get out and flip the outboard motor up and drag the boat along. It was hard work walking in this very shallow water. Something especially interesting were the rays. There were thousands and thousands of sting rays in that shallow water. As you walked along they wouldn't move until you were really close and then, all of a sudden, whoosh, they would take off. It was a little scary at times although I don't think they were dangerous. They weren't electric or anything like that.

Abu Dhabi is now a very prolific oil-producing sheikhdom. When we were there, one field, Murban, had been discovered in the '50s, but it was slow to be developed. The reason was that in drilling their first well they struck oil, of course, but because it is a carbonate reservoir, there is some sulphur or H2S present. They didn't realize this and, in doing some completion work on the first well, two engineers died from this H2S. So that scared them off. They didn't have any experience in drilling and completing in this kind of habitat then. They didn't come back to it for about eight years or so. Instead, they went off and drilled wells in other parts of Abu Dhabi. They did finally develop the Murban field and it was actually the first field to come on-stream. Geophysics picked up that one and then they had another big structure, Bu Hasa, just southwest of there. We discovered it just about the time I was there and I helped outline it – it is a big one. I think they thought it would be about an 18-billion-barrel field. The seismic data quality is okay down to a depth, but then lower down near the reservoir horizons it gets really shaky and you have to do some interesting extrapolations from up above to follow the deeper horizons. Later on, we did some digital work and that helped to improve the data quality.

Seismic data acquisition is always a bit of a problem in desert countries and it's done in different ways in Iran and Saudi Arabia. In Abu Dhabi we had our own system. We did mainly reflection work whereas a lot of the work in Iran was refraction – big surface type of thing. Some of the work in Saudi was refraction, but later they went to reflection. We usually had two crews working in Abu Dhabi. We drilled shallow holes with normal drill rigs. This meant we needed water to bring out the cuttings and getting water, of course, is always a problem in areas like that.

There are a couple of areas down in the south part of Abu Dhabi – in the Liwa, it's called – where sand dunes are 600 feet high. In parts of Saudi you can get them up to 800 feet high. The windward side of the sand dunes is quite navigable and the slopes not too great but the south – the leeward side of the dune – is quite steep and the angle of repose is somewhere around 30 degrees for that type of sand. You always work from the top down. Working from the bottom up on these slopes is pretty tough going. I've climbed a few of them and, given the rather poor condition I was in, found it really hard work. You'd go up a couple of steps and slide back one. The sand was very soft. Using vehicles to traverse the dunes, you wouldn't try to go straight up unless it was a little one, in which case you would take a run at it and your momentum would carry you up. But with the big ones, you would go around and come down from the back. Whenever we'd come across this kind of dune, we'd lay the cable and the geophones from the top down – we'd never go from the bottom up. To come down these things with a vehicle, you'd come to the top, stop and make sure you were at right angles to the edge of the dune. Then you would just ease it into 4-wheel drive and your lowest gear and it would more or less slide down. The sand would slide with you, making an eerie kind of sound. Of course, if you ever got your vehicle crosswise you could roll it over in this soft stuff.

Another hazard was in some places where the wind would swirl as it came over the top of the dune creating a kind of circular pit down below. You wouldn't drive into one of these on purpose, but if you came over the top and all of a sudden slid into one of these pits, you would get stuck at the bottom. Some of these potholes were so sharp from all sides that if you got down into one you'd had it. You just had to wait for people to come and pull you out.

Of course, losing people or having them not show up was a critical thing there. The crews would always be known to have gone out in a certain direction and when people strayed off that intended line that day, somebody would be notified. We had radios, of course, or a lot of us did, because if somebody didn't come back to where they should have been in a matter of hours, people started worrying and planning to go out to find them. They say 24 hours in the sun in the summertime is just it; after that you may be gone. So keeping track of where the vehicles were and where the people were was a constant problem. For instance, in Qatar the route from one side of the island to the other is fairly well populated but, even there, if the office on the east side sent somebody to the west side where the oilfield was, they would notify the west side that so and so was coming over and that he should be there at such and such a time. If he didn't arrive on schedule, they would communicate back and forth. If he didn't show up in a few hours, people would be sent out from both offices both ways to look for him. It wasn't as formal in the desert where we were working in the camp but if somebody didn't come in an hour or two after the crew came in, we'd turn the vehicles around and go on out to find him.

This could be a real problem. They say one fellow was out 24 hours and when they found him he was close to death. People new to the desert who don't know how to behave (get under the truck, keep a hat on and so forth) could get into trouble. When I was there, I remember a couple of accountants went out from the little office they had in Abu Dhabi to a rig that was drilling southwest of there. They did their accounting work and decided to go back to headquarters before it got dark. They started heading back to the main office but night came and they still hadn't arrived. There wasn't much anyone could do about it late at night but early the next morning they went out and found them. They had been travelling in the wrong direction, heading west towards Saudi Arabia.

Well, that's the Abu Dhabi seismic work. As I said, I had two crews and while I was in Bahrain, I would visit them every few weeks. This was from April through to May, 1962.

I headed home in early June to join the family in Edmonton. The intention was that we would have a short holiday there before heading back to Europe for a vacation I had coming before taking up a new posting with IPC, this time in England.

Chapter 6 – Europe and the Arab Emirates

In April, 1963, Mickey was promoted to Chief Geophysicist overseeing the Iraq Petroleum Company's operations in Qatar, Abu Dhabi and Dubai. Donna and David moved into a new home in Worcester Park near Epson and Trish went to a girls' boarding school. Mickey spent much of the next four years in the London office, directing geophysical operations in the three countries.

The kids finished their school year in Edmonton and then we went to the Continent to finish our vacation. I had about three months of leave coming to me. The Company was pretty liberal in their vacations policy because of the locations we worked in. So towards the end of June we headed from Edmonton to New York, visiting people in Regina we had known there on the way. We ended up in New York at the "Shabby Abbey" again and I checked in at the office at the headquarters of Standard Oil of New Jersey in the RCA building.

This time we were to go to Europe and pick up the car we had ordered from Mercedes in Frankfurt. It had been ready in March but, of course, we couldn't pick it up at that time as I was heading to Bahrain. We had a relative of a friend on the seismic crew in Baghdad who lived in Hamburg pick it up for us in Frankfurt.

We had arranged to travel to Europe by ship this time and we were booked on the France. However, the crew went on strike just a day or two after we got to New York. We thought we might have to change our plans and fly, but hung on for a few days. Finally, they settled the strike and we were able to embark on the liner – the new one, not the Isle de France, but the France, about July 5th. It had just been commissioned and it was a fantastic ship. We learned Dwight Eisenhower and Mamie were booked to sail on this ship but had cancelled their plans.

We had a lovely cabin for the four of us and the kids had play areas and chaperones and all that kind of stuff. There were movies all over the place. I remember that Spartacus was one movie we saw. Guess who was one of the leading men in it – Woody Strode, the fellow I'd played football with in Calgary in 1949. He had got to be quite a movie star and this was one of his better roles, playing the black gladiator the Roman Emperor finally knifed in the back.

It was a tremendous trip and we made some new friends. I still remember the name of one couple from St. Louis, Missouri – the Fielders. We had our formal clothes for the trip and there are some pictures of us having a gay time on the way over.

We landed in Cherbourg with a whole bunch of suitcases. Donna keeps saying we had thirteen or more, but I hope it wasn't that many. Anyway, from there we got up to Hamburg by train and met with the person who had picked up our Mercedes 220SE – supposedly brand new and with no mileage on it. I looked at the dial and saw "300" on one dial and I said, "Oh well, I guess he's put on 300 coming up here from Frankfurt". But it wasn't 300; it turned out to be 3000. This guy had gone up to Sweden twice, I think it was he said. I hadn't given him permission – he'd just done this on his own. That's the way some people are. Anyway, I claimed that he had messed it up more or less for good. It tended to overheat. Other than that it was a beautiful car. It was one of the new squarish models that came out after those late 1950s bustle-backs. The trunk was enormous. It was so big we could put those 13 suitcases Donna says we had in there. I don't think there were that many. Anyway, we had a lovely time – the two kids and us. By then they were old enough to enjoy it – both of them. This would have been the summer of 1962 so Patricia was 10 and David 8.

Figure 13: Donna and the kids, David and Patricia, 1962.

We had a lot of fun traveling through Germany and Denmark and back through France. We stayed in one hotel in the southeast part of Paris and the price of the two rooms for the four of us was almost the equivalent of the price of breakfast. I still have a copy of the bill to show people because it was pretty hard to believe. We could speak some French but not much. Tricia could speak a little bit, too, but hers was Canadian French and the French youngsters couldn't understand it very well.

We got back across the Channel to England on a ferry. We got good and sick because the Channel can get really rough at times. We hadn't bought too many things as we had so much of our own stuff. Later on you'll find out that, on our trips to Europe, we used to fill the car up with antiques. Sometimes we would have a bit of trouble getting it all through Customs on the way back – but this time we were okay. We had arranged to stay with friends who welcomed us into their house in Southfield which was about six miles north of Wimbledon. We unloaded and stayed there for a few weeks while we looked for a house of our own.

Of course, the housing situation in England was completely unlike anything we had been familiar with back on the Prairies. I started looking close to London but kept going further and further out. Finally, we got out to Worcester Park which is about six miles north of Epsom and found something there we could just manage. We bought a house that had been built in the 1930s. It was a solid brick house with nice grounds and a small single garage but it hadn't been upgraded since it was built. When we moved in I had to move the big oaken garage door six inches further out in order to get the Mercedes in lengthwise. It was a long car by British standards.

I had to go back to Bahrain by the end of September but we couldn't get into the house until October. I'd arranged for a contractor to do the things we wanted done before I left, hoping he would get in there soon. But things dragged on and on. I left for the Middle East while Donna and the kids stayed on with the Stonemans. They were friends we had first met in Brooks back in 1941. Harold Stoneman was a nice fellow. They were both originally from Springfield,

111

Missouri. They were good enough to keep the kids and Donna for what turned out to be a couple of months. Eventually the contractors got to work on the house and it was ready the end of October.

Donna and David moved into the house while the contractors were still finishing their work. We had settled Tricia into a girls' boarding school so she was taken care of. David we got into a boys' day school in Epsom. He would walk down to the station about three-quarters of a mile away, take the train to Epsom, get off there and walk up to his Kingston House school. Donna had a tough time, of course. There was no heat in the place so we were putting in central heating. Before that, their heating consisted of a hot water register in the central hall run off a stove in the pantry. We had that yanked out and gas-fired hot water central heating put in. We also had to redo the wiring. Then when the contractors were ripping up the floor in the living room they found some termites and that turned out to be another big problem. Donna had to have them fumigated out of there and the floor replaced. Eventually, by the end of November it was all done. By then it was getting quite cold.

I was still out in Bahrain, of course, and by the end of November I was going to come home for a short Christmas break and then go back out again. We had one of the biggest fogs for a long time in England towards the end of November and I had plane reservations to come into Heathrow. Well, the fog was so thick that flights to England were delayed again and again. Finally I got on a flight about the 7th of December that landed in Scotland. I took the train down to London and then out to the house. That was really a pea soup fog.

Donna had some stories about it. On one of the first days of the fog David got lost walking home from the train station.

When he finally got in around 5:30 or 6:00, much later than he should have, he was in tears. He had been lost – got befuddled. He was not quite nine at the time. We lived across the street from an Anglican church and the minister came over and talked to Donna about the conditions and said, "Well, enough of that." His boy was going to the same school. "I'll take the two boys down tomorrow," which he did and he took another fellow with them. Coming back, to make their way home, the other fellow walked in front of the car with a big electric torch to lead the way. That's how thick the fog was.

When I got home, Donna was upset by this and because I had not been around to help deal with the contractors. As it was, she really got to know English workmen. "Tea up" was the big thing of the day. About 10:30 or so the shout would be, "Tea up, Mrs. H." You know they had brewed the tea and the tea was ready – "Come on and have a cup of tea." She did what she could to help them, worked with them, and lived through all of that. It was quite a time in her life.

Figure 14: Donna entertaining at home in England, 1962

We spent Christmas together and early in January I went out to Bahrain again and did my thing there until March. By then they'd retired the previous geophysicist and put me in as the Chief Geophysicist of Iraq Petroleum Company. That's what I did for the next four years in Qatar, Abu Dhabi and Dubai. The routine for me, once I got back there, was to visit the crews and the operations in each area about three times a year and try to improve the quality of the data, evaluate things and write a report when I got home. I also did a lot of interpretation work myself. For instance, I did the interpretation of most of the data that was acquired in Abu Dhabi. I had another geophysicist, Nick Zylstra (who had met us in Baghdad back in 1960), helping me interpret. We did the interpretation and massaged that data back and forth and up and down. We located all the step-out development wells on Asab and a couple of other structures in Abu Dhabi. We also developed Bu Hasa which was about an 18-billion-barrel field. Asab had several billion in it and we developed that. I spotted all the step-out wells and hit the oil-water levels in the right porous part of the Jurassic reservoir.

Next we drilled one big feature near the border. It was a big structure. We figured this was the daddy of them all. For a time we held off drilling it because it was further down near the border with Saudi and we had enough oil in production closer in to satisfy all the needs. We finally drilled it just to make sure we got it before they decided to take the acreage away as they had done in Iraq. So we drilled this monster near the border and to our surprise the main horizons were water – wet. Luckily, we found oil in some other reservoirs where we hadn't quite expected it. Then, of course, I reworked the whole darned thing to try to figure out why this monstrous structure didn't have oil in the formations we were expecting to find it in. I did that analysis by reworking the history of the structure and the estimated migration time of the oil. I had shown that while that lower horizon oil was being generated and migrating, the structure was open to the southeast. Later, when the oil had migrated, the structure kept rising. By then the oil had gone by and been trapped somewhere in the south and east – in Saudi Arabia mainly. So, later on this five-kilometre border exchange might have been important as some of that five kilometres contained the oil that had spilled off to the southeast. Saudi now has an oilfield in that area – probably more than one. That was interesting work and it was quite a job to reconstruct it all.

That was about the last of the big interpretation jobs I did in that area. It was time to move on. I'd given them all the ideas I had and helped train their interpreters and geophysicists and I thought it was time to move on. The Iraq Petroleum Company's area of concessions was shrinking. We'd lost Iraq and Dubai by then. In Iraq all we were doing was producing some oil – not exploring. Other people were given acreage and that was another thorn in our side. One of the companies that owned Iraq Petroleum Company was the French Government Oil Company, CFP. Our chief negotiator in 1961-62 was the man on loan from them in Iraq and, of course, the first group that got any new acreage later on in Iraq was CFP. I assume they had all our maps and everything else and could pick up the best acreage. All this seemed a bit shady but that's the oil business, I guess.

During the 1962 to '65 period we made several trips to Europe, including one to visit my family's old village in Hungary in the summer of 1964.

Every one of these trips went through Paris where we had a little hotel that was recommended to us by a friend who had been there. It was right on the Champs-Elysées about 4 blocks down from the Etoile. It was called the Arromanches

115

Hotel and it was on Rue Chateau Briand – a little side street half a block off the Champs on the northeast side. It was a six-floor hotel with one little elevator. The owner was a former country gentleman, a Monsieur Gigot, who had bought the hotel with his retirement money. He was a wonderful man. We would drive there directly – right into Paris and to the hotel. Parking was awkward at times and I had one or two difficult episodes there. There was no parking right in front of the hotel but we'd drop off our suitcases and Donna would get those into the hotel while I would move off and try to find a place to park the car nearby. Once we got in we'd get our room which could be anywhere from the second floor on up to the sixth. The rooms were small – nothing glamorous – but adequate and most of them had bathrooms.

M. Gigot was really kind to us. I can remember money was always a problem because we hadn't wanted to take much money into England. If you brought in money from your supposedly current earnings, you had to pay tax on it if you were living there. Lower-salaried people would pay tax on 500 pounds a year; higher-salaried people – which would include foreigners – would pay tax on 1,000 pounds a year. But if you brought in a whole bunch of money – supposedly your current earnings – you would be taxed on it by the British authorities. Because of this we were always trying to avoid bringing money into England and tried to live off a minimum amount there. When we were travelling on the Continent, we would have money sent over from Canada to Paris, usually through American Express. I remember once we were planning a two-week vacation with the kids and we arrived in Paris with a minimum amount of money we'd brought from England. We got checked into the hotel and I went over to the American Express office – and found they had no money for us. This was on a Friday and I went back to the hotel feeling quite dejected. When he saw me, M.

Gigot said, "Oh, what's the matter, what's the matter? You look sad." I said, "Well, we don't have any money for the weekend, let alone the vacation we were planning." "Well," he said, " no problem. How much do you want?" He floated us two weeks' vacation money. That was pretty darned generous. Well, it so happened that Monday was a holiday so Tuesday we went down to American Express early and tried again. We looked through everything, under every name, in every slot and finally found it filed in the wrong place probably under "M" or something instead of "H". But over that whole weekend we lived off Gigot's money We went shopping at the flea market which was always the first place we would go because of Donna's interest in antiques, especially French antiques. We bought some stuff, of course, and, since we were going on with out vacation trip, Gigot said we could store it with him. So we moved whatever we had into his apartment on the ground floor, went on with our vacation and picked up the things we'd bought on the way back.

I remember another trip when we collected an awful lot of stuff. There were just the two of us this time and when we got back to Paris we had a couple of additional days to spend. Then it was time to pack up and go home and get through Customs. Well, you could bring in stuff that was over a hundred years old without any duty but anything that was less than 100 years old you had to pay duty on. We were aware of this and tried to buy only antique pieces. This time we had a big load of stuff and to get it in the Mercedes we had to take out the front passenger seat. That took some doing. You had to have a big screwdriver and I didn't have one. M. Gigot said, "No problem. I'll get my grandson here and he'll come and help you." So the grandson got his tools and came out and helped me get that huge seat out. We got it out and set it on the sidewalk. It was monstrous. Then we got the furniture down and packed it into the car. We had a big commode with legs and a marble top. Well, I took the backseat out, too, and we put the marble top vertically in the back seat area and then on the empty right side of the vehicle we fed this commode through the right side door. Unlike doors on North American cars, the Mercedes doors would open up to right angles from the car and not stop at the 70- or 80-degree angle. Consequently, we could swing the commode in, pivot it around the right side pillar between the front and back door and put it in upside down lengthwise where I'd taken the back seat out. After that the other stuff went on top, in the backseat, and in the trunk. There was a little bucket seat about a foot wide that we could put in beside the driver and that was where Donna sat when we started back. For the rest of the load, we had a one-meter French bed we thought was antique. We got almost all of it in the trunk but the bed slats had to be pivoted around inside the vehicle and rested on top of the commode. The foot and the headboard had fit into the trunk except about six inches of the top of the headboard which was ornately carved in the Louis XV style. It stuck out of the trunk so I had to leave the trunk opened and padded so it wouldn't bounce on this antique headboard.

In 1964 we made another trip to the Continent which included a visit to my old home village in Hungary. As usual, we stopped in Paris and stayed at our favourite hotel a couple of days. I think the next stop was Strasbourg. We went out that night with the kids to Maison Kammersal, a typical old French-German establishment. The house was narrow at the bottom, then larger on the way up. There was a bar downstairs, a restaurant on the second floor and then lodging higher up. We had a huge meal of typical mixed German/French Strasbourg fare – sauerkraut, smoked meat and sausages. They served all four of us on a huge platter; then we were given plates, and we dug in. It was very tasty. The place was right next to the cathedral that had only one spire and we wondered what had happened to it. Apparently it had not been finished centuries ago. Right in the middle of Strasbourg.

Then we went on to Vienna. Traveling in the Mercedes was quite comfortable. We had a reservation there in a very nice small hotel. Donna and I went out that evening and had a bit of fun. We had a few dances. The hotel provided a baby-sitter so the kids were well taken care of. I can remember coming home. We'd really boozed it up and I remember wandering down the road instead of taking a taxi until we finally found the hotel. The next day we drove on into Hungary. We were a little apprehensive as the borders were at that time closed and tightly controlled. We had the proper papers but I was a little worried, this being my first visit back since 1929.

How would we be received? Well, as we approached the border we could see towers up ahead, fences, and the flash of the sun on metal. There were guards there in the tower and the sun was shining on their rifles. We got to the first gate and they opened that up, but as soon as we got in, the huge metal gate bar clunked behind us and there we were in between two massive metal bars twenty feet long. Up above was the guard tower and the guard had his rifle trained on you. The border people came out and I had to go in. Everything had to be inspected, including everything in the car. I think I had enough papers to satisfy them so they opened up the front gate and let us in but it was quite a worrisome entry into Hungary. We then drove to the village just about seventy kilometres on the other side of Budapest – northeast near the Czech border in the low hills running east-west. We located our Uncle John who had been in Canada twice. He was married to my mother's sister and we had known them in Canada. They had a son, Alex, alive and well, a year or two older than me. They had been back and forth to Canada twice so he was all mixed up in his education and language. Uncle John was a real "pinko" – more Red than pink – and he'd taken the money he'd gotten for his farm lands near Brooks in Canada back to Hungary. I think he gave a good portion of it to the Russian cause although I don't know how they managed that sort of thing.

There was a big celebration going on in Budapest. Khrushchev was there for the twentieth anniversary of the "Russian liberation" of Hungary. Uncle John, being a real supporter of the Russian cause, had been awarded the Red Star that night so had the Star on his chest. We stayed in his house and enjoyed the hospitality. Alec and his wife were there and she was very interesting. I remember her taking Donna out and showing her various things while I was with Alec, mainly. One night Uncle John had some friends over and we all had a few drinks and everybody got jolly. Every time somebody lifted a glass everybody would take a drink. I wasn't familiar with this system so I'd pick up my glass and so everybody else would lift theirs. We didn't toast something every time, but whenever you picked up a glass, everybody had a drink so we were all getting pretty well along. I remember later on Donna asked Uncle John to sing the Hungarian national anthem. That created a big to-do. Of course, there were two anthems – the old one that I remembered and a new Russian one – the Communist one. They all argued, of course, and Uncle John wanted to sing the new one. Some of the old guys objected and they sang the old one for Donna. I was quite pleased as it was a much better song than the new one. I don't know what they sing now.

One other incident took place about a day after we'd arrived. There was a knock on the door and a couple of plainclothes guys came in to remind me that I was supposed to report to the police inside of 24 hours from the time I'd arrived. I had known that, but forgot. As it turned out, with Uncle John's help and a drink or two, things were smoothed over. I don't know that I should say so, but all through history – and this is folklore and current lore – the Hungarian Secret Police were the cruelest, possibly equaling or even surpassing the infamous KGB. I don't know whether it's that way today but, at any rate, that's what I have heard.

We visited around the village and saw the old house I was born in and had lived in for five years. We had all been awarded our share of that house – the biggest in the town – and I guess it brought a pretty good price, the commercial values for business purposes being pretty good. The proceeds were divided seven ways. Grandpa Stephen had seven children – four boys and three girls – so it was divided seven ways and then our share was divided five ways so I ended up with one thirty-fifth of the value of the house, which wasn't very much, especially when you converted it to the Canadian dollar or the UK pound. So when the house was sold, I asked them to give my share to Irvin, the son of my Dad's second wife. (After Mom died in 1948, Dad had gone back and married the widow of his brother who had died early, just a couple of years after coming home from being in prison in Siberia. However, she would not leave Hungary without her son, Irvin, and they wouldn't let Irvin leave Hungary at that time – for whatever reason they had. They'd let the wife out – a married lady – but they wouldn't let the soldier-aged male out. So she would not come out for years. It wasn't until much later that she changed her mind and joined Dad in Canada.) I met Irvin and I gave him the proceeds of my one thirty-fifth share of our house in Matramindszent.

I did visit the old house but I think it had been converted into a pub then. It really didn't look much like the house I had lived in as it had been changed a lot. But the huge oven in the middle where the food used to be cooked was still there. (On another visit, in 1979, the house had become a big village store.)

We visited others of the family in the east end of town where a couple of our relatives lived – Irvin and Dad's brother. Grandfather had been mayor for donkeys' years and when he passed away his son, Andy, was made mayor. He was a very pleasant fellow who enjoyed life and always had a twinkle in his eye. He was different from Father or Gabriel, the second son, that I knew back in Canada. I think the village thought highly of him because he had guided them through the period of German oppression during the Second World War and then during the period of the Russian influence for nearly 20 years and then through the so-called Revolution of 1956 and beyond.

We had a good time but I recall one worrisome incident. When we were driving around the village in this beautiful Mercedes (everyone wanted a ride in it, of course), the roads were very, very poor. One of the properties we were driving into had a gatepost with a high pin in the middle. I didn't realize how high it was and how low my car's steering gear was so this gear got caught and bent a little bit. Cousin Alec was around at the time and he said, "Oh, we'll fix that." So he got underneath and bent it a bit and said, "Well, try it now." I tried it but he remained underneath because the gear was still groaning. It was partially fixed, but it groaned and creaked all the way back to England. I finally took it down to the Mercedes people and they fixed it.

In Hungary, when visitors are leaving, everybody gives you a present. Everybody. One of the favourite presents is a small bottle of Slivovich which, as you know, is a very poorly refined alcohol from plums. It was pretty God-awful stuff. Maybe you could stand the alcohol part of it, but the smell was terrible. We had a whole lot of these bottles and I stuck them away every place I could. We weren't going to drink it, but we thought we might be able to do something about it back in England. As we drove along we came upon a work crew having lunch alongside the road. They had a fire going and were cooking their bacon and onions on a stick and dripping the fat onto bread. I had some other food, including some chicken, so I stopped and took it all over to them, including the Slivovitch. I could communicate a little bit so I explained we could not handle all of this and invited them to be our guests. They were quite pleased. Unfortunately, one bottle was hidden somewhere and showed up back in Worcester Park. It took years to get rid of this stuff. Eventually, one of my Norwegian friends from Baghdad thought it was OK and drank it.

We got out of Hungary on that trip without much trouble except that at the border they still searched the vehicle (underneath, the trunk, everywhere) before they let us through. I don't know what they were looking for. When we got back to the West our first stop along the way was Vienna which wasn't far from the border. We didn't have any accommodation, but thought we'd like to stay at this fancy hotel, get cleaned up and get the car cleaned, too. It was a horrible mess because of the poor facilities back at Matramindszent. So we arrived at this beautiful palace-like hotel, drove up the ramp, stopped and said we'd like to stop for the night. The doorman said, "You just go on in and I'll take care of the car." I said, "Well, it's pretty dirty." And he said, "Yes, it is, and needs cleaning." So he took the car and we went into this beautiful hotel. We got cleaned up and came down to the restaurant in this beautiful place. We saw a little bit more of Vienna. We had seen it before, I recall, I

123

guess in '62 when we'd picked the car up. It was a really nice stop there. And the hotel returned a sparkling clean car!

Despite the creaky steering, we got home, back through Paris. We didn't carry many antiques that time.

The next year, in May of 1965, we made another trip, this time to a geophysical convention in Madrid. I'd joined the European Geophysical Society and there was a meeting in Madrid, May, 1965. We decided we'd take the kids along and again visited Paris, our favourite place. Then we drove on down the east coast into Spain and along the south coast. We had accommodation at Marbella, west of Malaga, in a lovely, fairly new hotel. There were only a few hotels there at the time. The little town nearby had a bull ring like most of the towns. We took the kids down to see that, but they were not too impressed with bull fighting. Apart from that it was just a nice quiet break – not too busy, not too touristy but while we were there a bunch of Germans arrived, looking at property to buy. This was in 1965.

We then headed back east then straight north to Madrid and into our accommodation there. I attended the convention for five days. I was surprised by how backward the presentation equipment was. The operator was not used to all these slides being handed to him so it was kind of laughable at times. But I guess it was their first attempt at holding a geophysical convention. I recall being at a geophysical convention in New Orleans back in 1956 and, of course, by then such conventions in the States were run pretty smoothly – especially in New Orleans with all that entertainment they had to offer.

The Geophysical Society had been formed in the 1930's in the States so by '56 they'd gone through many conventions and could handle them pretty well. They could handle as many as 5000 delegates. Anyway, after this convention in Spain we headed home. We stopped along the way, staying at some beautiful haciendas. You could do this for five dollars a person in those days. The food was always good and, of course, the wine was, too. I don't think we brought back much that trip, with the kids along, not nearly as much as when there were just the two of us.

We were getting near the end of our stay in England and my work with the Iraq Petroleum Company. Where to next? Of course, in the last few months I'd been thinking about this a lot. There had been several offers. One was from Imperial Oil who said they would like me to come back to fill a position they had available. I also had a chance to go to New York to the headquarters of Esso Exploration Group. They handled all the exploration on land and offshore for the holding company, Standard Oil of New Jersey – as the name was then. In the end, I decided on the New York job. That was at the end of March, 1967.

In between finishing up my time with IPC and taking up the New York job there was the Geological Congress in Mexico City which was held during the first week of April, 1967. The Company and, in particular, my boss, Dr. Thiebeaud, appreciated what I had done for them and he arranged for me to present a paper on Abu Dhabi at this Congress. So I spent the last couple of months with IPC working on this paper about new oil areas in the Abu Dhabi sheikhdom. I got help from all the people involved and did all the right things. Then I sent the paper to the chairman for my panel for these new oilfields, an Iranian named Nafisi. Then I went out for my last trip to the Middle East. By the time I got back the story was that Nafisi had said that I couldn't present my paper at the Congress because there were two figures that had the Persian Gulf named the Arabian Gulf.

Here is how this happened. On the Iraq - Saudi Arabia - Trucial Coast side, the governments wanted us to refer to that body of water as the 'Arabian Gulf.' So everything we did had 'Arabian Gulf' all over it. We always referred to the 'Arabian Gulf' – never 'Persian Gulf.' But, no, this chairman of the panel from Iran said it had to be 'Persian Gulf'. This has been a big issue there for donkeys' years. So I said, "Fine, I'll just change those two figures and put in 'Persian Gulf' on it for your benefit." But he refused and said it couldn't be done – a typical Iranian. Consequently, I couldn't give this paper at the Congress. We went to the Congress and I participated in all the other events. My paper was published by the Congress, but it wasn't given orally. I can remember sitting there with this panel and one of the Iraqi delegates standing up and saying "I see that there are several papers that are not being given. Can we have the reasons for this?" There were two other papers where the same thing happened – the authors had put in the Arabian Gulf on their figures. That was typical of the conflict between Iraq and Iran – or the Arabs versus the non-Arabs. This had gone on, of course, all through our time there. For instance, I never did get into Iran. I got to the border and looked across, but that was as far as I got. To get to Iran you had to go to Bahrain and from Bahrain you needed a special visa to go to Iran. Then, of course, you couldn't have a page in your passport showing that you'd been to Iran when you got back to this side!

Chapter 7 – New York and Houston

In the spring of 1967 Mickey and the family left England and resettled near New Canaan, Connecticut. Mickey worked in the Esso Exploration offices in downtown Manhattan as a Geophysical Advisor. They remained there until the fall of 1970 when they moved again, this time to Houston, Texas, where Mickey served as Geophysical Advisor for Esso Exploration.

New York

We packed up everything in UK and sold our house there at a modest profit. We went to the Geophysical Congress in Mexico City on the way from England to New York. We spent a week in Mexico attending the Congress and taking a number of side trips. The kids were with us and we got around as much as we could – we all suffered from the Mexican "problem." At the end of the convention we took a trip down to a little place in the southeast called Posa Rica where one of their first important oil fields was located.

We couldn't go directly to New York from there due to US immigration laws so we had to over-fly the States to Toronto and then fly to New York. The people in New York didn't understand this and weren't too happy as I was already a week late and now there was another day's delay. But I arrived there on a Tuesday instead of a Monday and reported to the office. We stayed for a couple of days at the Shabby Abbey.

Then we had to find a place to live. While my salary was pretty good, when you took into account the cost of living in New York, it wasn't that great. You had to look out of town and keep going until you found a place from which you could commute. We settled on New Canaan in

127

Connecticut in a little area called Silvermine and bought a new house on two and a half acres, part of an eight or nine acre plot that was divided four ways. I was chosen to be the guy to look after the gravel road that came into these properties. That took a bit of work.

We got settled there. The kids were admitted into New Canaan High School. This was the spring of 1967 and by then, of course, the kids in school were into the drug scene. Our two had their first experience with drugs there, especially son David.

Donna and I kept our noses to the grindstone as, with the cost of the mortgage on the house, we didn't have extra money. I didn't join a golf club and didn't have a single golf game while I was there (three and a half years). Donna fixed up the interior of the new house and I did a lot of work cleaning up around it.

During the second summer there I spent my five-week vacation working on the property. It was a good size, wooded, with a new house with lots of debris scattered around. I cleaned up all the old wood, splitting it and carting it back into the basement for firewood. Getting rid of the skunk cabbage took weeks. I'd be out there at eight in the morning, go in for a bite of lunch, work until five, go back in for a drink – and we didn't go out. That's the way it went for most of the first five weeks. I didn't spend much money except on what I needed for the grounds work.

The property had been owned by Barnard Baruch's secretary and had a tall picket fence all round it. This was in a state of disrepair so I took it apart and burned it. Our property was hidden from the road by a big old graveyard where early settlers were buried. I kept this fire going for

128

days, burning all that crud that had been lying around on the property for years.

I was kept busy at home and going to the office. I'd leave the house at 6:20 in an old beaten-up Chevy and drive down to the station. Then I would catch the train for the hour or so trip into the city, walk through Grand Central and then on to the office. I walked all the time except for the time when I broke my leg. We were supposed to be there from eight thirty until five, but each guy had his own schedule due to the train situation. Those trains on the Connecticut and New Haven Railway were terrible. They'd break down any number of times. If a train broke down going into the office in the morning that was OK because it was on the Company's time. but when there was a breakdown going home, you wouldn't get home until eight or nine sometimes and that was on your own time! So the routine was that, if there was a breakdown in the evening, you tried to catch a ride of some kind rather than sit there for who knows how long.

This commuting became really tough when I broke a bone in my foot and dislocated my ankle skiing. It happened on a weekend in the north of Connecticut. I wasn't a good skier and I was using my son's old boots and skis. I came down the hill, hit some ice, and went into a snow bank at the side. The harness didn't release, a bone snapped and I dislocated my ankle. I didn't know what to do. I tried to ski down the hill on one ski but when that didn't work, I tried to walk down. It was pretty steep and I damaged the ankle even more. It wasn't until I got to the bottom that I found a ski patrol. They put me on their toboggan, took me to an emergency shelter and put a temporary cast on it. The next day I got to a doctor in New Canaan and got a regular major cast put on. It went all the way from my toes right up to my waist. It was a crooked cast in order to put the ankle back in line.

The next day I started commuting to work with this huge cast on. My daughter would take me down to the station. I'd have my satchel over my shoulder and I'd grab the bars of the railway car, hoist myself up on the high step and she'd give me a heave into the car – with my crutches, of course. Then I'd try and find a seat. Once or twice I couldn't find a seat and had to stand the whole way into New York. Nobody got up to offer me their seat. I remember once an old lady saw a seat the same time I did and she and I raced for it and she won! So I stood.

Once we got into the city I'd get through Grand Central and try to find a cab. Of course any guy with two good legs could usually beat me to the cab. Finally I'd get one to pick me up and take me the few blocks to the office. For the two weeks I had to use cabs, very few of the cabbies would get out of the cab and open the door for me. Picking me up, they would just sit there until I could get into the back of the cab, get my crutches and satchel in and try to reach the door handle to pull it shut past my leg in the crooked cast. After the five-minute trip to the office, I'd get out the best way I could and they'd expect a tip for doing nothing. It was exasperating. But after two weeks I got the big cast off and a walking cast put on so then it was easier. Then I took two buses, one up north and then I would cross over a couple of blocks on another bus which took me fairly close to the Radio City Music Hall where the office was. It was a big relief when I could do that. This went on for a full month.

I remember the first day in the office with the cast on. It was a Tuesday and I went for the normal lunch down the thirty-one flights on my crutches, perspiring and tired from a lot of work, across the road to the RCA building, down a long hall to the elevators, up to the 64th floor and then along to the dining room. I was pooped. But I'd have my lunch and then start back, down the hall, across the road, down another hall and up the thirty-one floors to my office. By the time I got to my office I was exhausted, so I decided to ask one of the guys teo just bring me a sandwich. I did this until I got my walking cast. Then I was able to go for my own lunch up on the 64th floor again. (The Company lunch room – no charge).

I did make one trip to Houston with crutches and full cast. That was quite a plane trip, but I got there, did what I had to do and got home again. I remember one of the stewardesses remarking on what a nice cologne I had on. It wasn't cologne, it was deodorant and sweat!

There was so much work to be done in the New York office that you had to take work home. On a normal commute you'd work on your way home. Then you would work again after dinner and do some more on the way back to the office next morning. I had the responsibility of supervising all the geophysical work, giving them advice and so forth, and then presenting the reports that the various districts sent in. These were mainly proposals they were making for acquisition of acreage, etc. I'd have to bone up on these , understand them and then present them to the board in New York. Believe me, that was a lot of work. But it was the same for everyone. If you didn't work at home you were in real trouble. You had to be a wizard with a photographic memory to do the job. Personnel was also a proper part of the job. To man those offices we had to be involved in recruiting personnel from all the various offices in the States and Canada.

Technically, you had to be abreast of everything that was going on. Most of this work was off-shore. I'd done very little of this so there was a lot of catching up to do that way. It was a tough few years and, to make it even tougher, this group was very unlike those I had been used to with Imperial Oil and Iraq Petroleum. They were loud, voluble, mostly American. I had a tough time there. I remember one guy saying, "Come on, Hajash, you never say anything." And I said, "For God's sakes, you guys are so loud, you don't give me a chance. Give me a chance and I'll say something." That sort of got me going. I guess I was a little bashful and hesitant.

Of course we had to make many trips to various offices. One was in Coral Gables, Florida. We had some work in South America but not an office there. We had work, of course, in Australia – the Gippsland Basin was just getting going. We had made our first discovery just about then. We also had an office in Singapore and another in Barcelona for the European area. We had another group in London so there were a lot of visits to be made. I made many trips in my first five years. I went around the world twice and I visited different offices at different times for specific reasons. So there was a lot of traveling. Our overall president for Esso exploration lived in Coral Gables. He'd get to New York on a Monday, spend a few days in the office and away he'd go to some other offices. He was always away on trips. He'd finally end up in Coral Gables again, then go back into the office and start the game all over again.

Most of the others spent a lot of time traveling also. We had three negotiators who spent their time negotiating and acquiring our acreages. The geologists were always on the go and sometimes we went together, sometimes not. I can remember two trips to Australia. I went out to some offshore rigs there. We traveled by helicopter and I remember one time they had a couple of press people out there and the tail rotor came off and decapitated the two of them. There was always some hazard in all of this.

That's the way the first three years went. There were lots of geophysical trips which involved visits to geological outcrops to review seismic operations. Then there would be discussions in the offices in these places; their problems, the techniques and the results obtained. Plans, budgets, personnel all would be discussed. Then you would get home, present the results to management and get ready for the next trip.

I remember sometimes taking my suitcase on the train to Grand Central. I'd put it in storage there and then, after work, come back to Grand Central, pick up my luggage, and head up to the roof. They had a helipad there and you'd wait until your chopper arrived to whisk you out to Kennedy Airport. I remember the chopper would rev up and then it would drop over the edge of the building – forty or so storeys – drop down to gain momentum and then take off for Kennedy. It was scary and exciting the first time. That was the quickest way to get to Kennedy. I did that a few times. Sometimes you'd go from your house straight to Kennedy by hired transport and get back home the same way. Kennedy was always the take-off place. Sometimes I would go down to Houston where we had a research centre – Esso Research. They did a lot of work for us – researching exploration, data processing and what have you.

In the fall of 1970 I had a special short assignment in the UK where I took over the office for two or three months, the manager being on a long leave. At the end of that, my wife and daughter came over and we went on that trip down through France and Spain.

Houston

After that little stint in the UK we moved from New York to Houston. We drove down in the Mercedes and put our other vehicle (a Volkswagen Beetle) in a van with our household stuff. We left David, as he hadn't finished high school. He was halfway through grade twelve. He stayed on in our house – which had been sold –until Christmas when he came down and joined us in Houston. We had an interesting drive down across Florida and Louisiana into Texas and to Houston.

We managed to buy a house in the west part of Houston just off Memorial Drive, one of the main thoroughfares. There was a golf course nearby and Memorial Park. We bought a house in a little village called Piney Point. There were about six villages in the west part of Houston. All were separate from Houston, with their own water, etc. We had our own steering group. It was a very nice house but it needed a lot of work. I remember the first long weekend was American Thanksgiving and we put eight gallons of paint on the inside. Trish was with us but all she did was run out and get more paint, more paint. The walls just soaked it up and, as a matter of fact, we discovered when we took the curtains down, the walls behind them had never been painted. They had just painted around the curtains. One window had a hole in it and you could tell by the edges that it was a bullet hole fired from the inside out. So the lady who lived there before had fired at a burglar or somebody through that window. I think we just left it there.

We put in a swimming pool. The reason was that when you sold a house and bought a new one, if you didn't spend as much on the new house as you got for your old one you'd have to pay tax on the difference. So we put in the pool and that made up the difference between what we got from our house up in Connecticut and what we paid for this one. So, no income tax there. Your own house is not tax-free in the US. You pay income tax on the capital gains.

Office work in Houston was the same as in New York – very strenuous and long hours. There were still trips around the world to the various offices I have mentioned and then, of course, we were there in the home territory of Humble Oil, the Standard Oil of New Jersey U.S. affiliate. In 1972 the latter became Exxon Corporation and Humble Oil became Exxon U.S.A.

In 1972 we had a big change in our hierarchy. Exploration brought in a new fellow who was going to change everything. Things weren't going well according to him, and he swept out a few of us and brought in his own cronies – Humble people, of course. I was replaced by another chief geophysicist and a couple of other fellows were also replaced. For a while I continued at the job. All the managers below this guy had a heck of a time running their own operations. All they were doing was putting out the fires this top boss had started. They were just working from day to day. There was no planning and all they were doing was jumping at his command and running around and asking us in a few minutes to have this, have that. It was a terrible situation. After a few months of this I was shipped off to a big research organization in the city there. I was being retreaded technically. I spent two years at Exploration Research.

The Exploration Research office was closer to the house, but the traffic was even worse than to the other office. I dug in there. I was familiar with the group and the work from previous work and they gave me some big projects. The first one was the migration type – trying to figure out some way to migrate our seismic data. When you acquire seismic reflection data, the reflections don't always come from

135

directly underneath. It is only when there is no dip in the geological bed that your reflection would come from underneath, so we were trying to figure out a simple way to get it back to the position these reflections came from.

I spent a good year on this project. A lot of darned hard work, working with their technical people, getting results, doing evaluation and going from there. In the end we made a big report on this program showing what we'd done, whether it was good or not, and whether we should use it until we could get something better – an automatic method. It was very awkward and labour-intensive. It was a big report and took about an hour and a half to present to the technical people and the others invited.

I worked on several other projects. The biggest involved data from Malaysia having to do with the "bright spot" evaluation. The intensity of the reflections from the sub surface is due to the velocity-density change at the various geological boundaries and/or other changes in the sediments in the sub-surface. Some of the oil companies and some geophysicists had found that the velocity of the sediment bed is affected to a large extent by the quantity of gases or air mixed in with the fluid, water and/or oil. This effect can be quite dramatic. Going from sediment with water to sediment with as low as five per cent gas in the mixture could lower the velocity of the sediment. The velocity change in that sediment is remarkable. About five per cent gas in the fluid in that porous bed can affect the velocity by ten to twenty per cent. Around five per cent gas in the fluid results in the lowest velocity. The change from water-laden porous sediment to a small percentage of gas results in a big change in velocity so you get a big change in the reflectibility of the bed which results in a "bright spot". This decrease in velocity within the bed results in a "time" low on the horizons below.

Our company was not aware of this. I had suspected something peculiar going on long ago in my Canadian work in the muskeg. As I have said, I was a shooter on a seismic crew back in the summers of the early 1940's when I was going to university. We measured the velocity of the wave from the blast source to a geophone that was always planted nearby – on the surface. Surprisingly, where the near surface velocity with normal water drilling fluid was about 5000 feet per second, the velocity in some of these shot holes was much lower. I couldn't understand this. I reasoned that there must be some error in the measuring of this time to the surface geophone. But as it transpired, much later, we came to understand that it was the mixture of the sediment and air in that very porous muskeg that lowered the velocity from the normal 5000 feet per second probably down to 3000-4000 feet per second or less.

The change in velocity was enough to change the reflectibility of the beds and the velocity of the wave traveling through the sedimentary section. This resulted in the marked change in the reflections from a low amplitude reflection to a high amplitude reflection. Some interpreters eventually understood this phenomenon. I had read reports by some academics who would talk theoretically about this velocity change but most people didn't pay much attention. Others thought it was just some lab report by a "research type". They thought it couldn't be right. Mobil Oil was one of the first companies to understand the effect and make use of this "bright spot" phenomenon.

At the Exxon Research lab I worked on the Malaysian data including the first gas-oil well there, Pulai # 1. I had worked on velocities for many years by then. I had also read all the related data I could get my hands on. With this background of seismic, geological, and geophysical knowledge and the data from Pulai #1, I was able to show that indeed the Pulai oil field had a "bright spot" signature starting from near sea bottom down. (Several of the oil and gas fields in the Malaysian eastern offshore basin had such a marked "time low" that we had a problem convincing Petronas (the Malaysian government oil company) that we were still drilling on the gas-oil field). I concluded that this change in reflectibility was mainly due to this effect and later on it turned out to be true.

I made a report to Research of my conclusions at a meeting that our Esso Exploration personnel attended. It was new to them and not accepted very well. Later, I made a report to a larger group including Humble geophysicists – they were just as sceptical. I showed them the "bright spots" (changes from water to gas or gas-oil mixture) but cautioned that this could mean a change from a porous water-filled bed to one filled with perhaps only five per cent gas – which was nowhere near economic by our terms. Perhaps it would have been in Japan where they were producing water to get the two to three per cent gas out of it to use for fuel but it was not economic in our normal oil business as we saw it. We needed a percentage of gas close to a hundred per cent to be economic. But our people insisted that all those "bright spots" meant a big change from water to a hundred per cent oil or gas-filled, porous sediment beds.

I took these same results to Malaysia on a special trip to show the work I had done on their data. They were also a little dubious. (I didn't know at that time that I would be posted there some six months later.) Then I went on over to the UK. I'd done some work for them on the North Sea data. I reported on that but also showed them this "bright spot" – low, variable gas percentage effect in sediments. Later, both offices received the data and the formal report

138

and benefited from it. That was the last big trip I took from the Houston Esso Exploration office.

Most of the exploration data resulting from the reflection seismic "time" data are presented in depth. Predicting the velocity to the various time horizons can be a very complex problem. The seismic data itself can be of poor quality because of this gas effect (whether only five per cent or more). This poorer quality data thus lowers the reliability of the velocity calculated. The resulting depth map can be less than reliable. A "time" low on the reflection horizon mapped can be a "structural" high and a desirable drilling location. However, a good technical approximation of velocities together with well data, if available, and change in the reflection amplitude ("bright spot") will usually improve the reliability of the predictions. In some oil-gas fields, the outline of various gas-oil prone zones can be (and have been) mapped with the aid of these "bright spots". This is so even if the hydrocarbons are trapped stratigraphically.

After two years at Research, I got a new posting to Malaysia. They were getting new offices in Kuala Lumpur but the operation field office was in Singapore. That's where the next posting was for six weeks.

So here was another big change in my career – one more time.

Chapter 8 – Singapore and Kuala Lumpur

In the fall of 1974 Mickey and Donna moved to Singapore where Mickey served briefly as Chief Interpreter for Esso Production Inc. before moving up to the Company's new office in Kuala Lumpur.

Malaysia

We had to terminate everything in Houston, sell the house and what have you and say goodbye to our friends. David had finished high school and gone back to Canada. He didn't want to go to university – neither of the kids did. Trish had taken some Dental Assistant training in Houston and David went back and started working in the oil fields in Alberta. So both were gone. Trish took our Beetle back to Canada with her plus furniture we'd given them. Donna and I sold the house at a nice profit. In the U.S. you have to have a tax clearance to leave the country so we paid our capital gains tax on the 2 houses we had owned there. I remember it was touch and go getting a tax clearance from the tax people in the States. But we got it, sold the car and took the plane to Victoria where Donna's folks now lived.

Just before that, Trish, who had gone up there a little earlier, got engaged. Donna went up to visit in May or June of 1974. Trish and her fiancé wanted to get married – or Donna talked them into getting married – so they called me to come up for the wedding. I said, "I'm not coming," but they talked me into it so I went up for her wedding and spent a few days there. Then Donna and I went back to Houston and at the end of August we finally moved from there back to Victoria on the way to Singapore. After a brief stay in Victoria, where we invested our money in some real estate, we took off for Singapore. I might mention that the exchange rate between the US dollar and Canadian was not in our favour at the time and there was a ten per cent discount to bring it into Canada. So when I got back to Canada I had ten per cent less. Nevertheless, we invested in some property in the Victoria area and took off. Of course, we had a dog at that time, a Yorkie named "George", and we had to arrange for transporting him out to Singapore and that was a big problem.

In those days very few airlines allowed dogs in the cabin or even on the plane at all, but in this case somehow we managed to take the dog in the cabin with us and he traveled to Singapore with us. Of course there was no place to go to the bathroom so the dog suffered, but he never had an accident on the plane. It was always such a relief when he was able to get out of the plane and onto the ground.

When we arrived in Singapore we had to put the dog in quarantine right away and that was for about a month. The place we put him had sort of a zoo-like atmosphere. It wasn't really a dog place but had a whole bunch of other animals including orangutans. We stayed in a nice hotel in Singapore – the Shangri-La, I think it was called. We were able to keep the dog with us in the hotel for the last two weeks. The manager said it would be OK as long as he didn't bark, etc. He was a very well-behaved dog. Donna used to take him in an airline carry-bag down in the elevator to a grassy area. They had a three-hole golf course on the grounds.

We stayed there six weeks. I was the Senior Interpreter and had a large staff of other interpreters working for me – mainly Americans, a few Canadians, some local Chinese and Malaysians.

After six weeks we moved up to Kuala Lumpur and again lived in a hotel until we got our housing arranged. The hotel was near a sports center where they had a race track but no horses. From our hotel window on Saturday afternoon we could see these people go down and sit in the stands. They'd all stand up and cheer, and then things would be quiet for a while and then they'd all stand up and cheer and carry on again. Then they'd get up and go somewhere and half an hour later they would be back, jumping up and down and cheering in the stands. We finally found out they were going down to place their bets or pick up their winnings somewhere and then would return to the stands. They were listening to the results of the races on an intercom of some kind. But there were no horses. It was kinda funny.

Housing was a little different in KL. We didn't buy our own homes. The Company rented them and then sublet them to us. All we had to say was "Yes" or "No" to the houses they offered us. We got a nice, normal house in a quiet area in the southeast of KL. It turned out to be about a mile and a half from the biggest golf course around, but it was a difficult course to get into. I had applied for membership during the trip I'd made the previous spring, giving them details of my work and all. It was a beautiful course. Donna managed to get in easily – as lady members could. But it took me four years before I could get in. Oh, I played there when invited by other members but I didn't become a member until 1979. In the meantime, I had joined a small Armed Forces course which accepted me right away. It was a little nine-hole course at the old British Forces base that included the military airport. We were able to take a few friends out so we had lots of golf on Saturday mornings, I remember. We'd be out at six a.m., choose up sides, and after the game there was lots of beer – very cheap Armed

Forces beer. Most of the time the weather was hot –boiling hot – so you needed a lot of fluid.

We had an office in what was once a big grocery store that hadn't survived so our people took it over. It included a huge 'fridge room and that became our vault and storage room for our data. We worked there for about a year. The office was not too far from the house. We bought a car and we shared cars to get to and from the office. We would have lunch in nearby little restaurants.

The exploration work was really interesting. Completely different geology, a different setting, and gosh – just different. We had Americans and other guys working there and lots of Chinese as well. The Chinese were about forty per cent of the population. But then we also had to hire the bumi putra. [Bumi putra translates literally as children of the soil and refers to the Malays and the tribal peoples of Malaysia – Ed.] They were not as sharp as the others, as a matter of fact. Higher education was a real problem in Malaysia and a few years before that, in 1969, they had a big to-do between the bumi putra and the Chinese with quite a bit of rioting and so on. Of interest, the bumi putra had their own university. Finally the government decided to make a new law regarding education, specifying how many spots had to be made available to the bumi putra. Because the Chinese were all sharper, they had previously tended to take up all the spots. Now the government, which was now mainly bumi putra (I think this was how it was set up when the British left in 1958 or 1959), insisted on places being made available for the bumi putra. There were very few Chinese members of government. The Chinese ran all the businesses so "of course" they had all the money. So there was always a lot of conflict between the bumi putra and the Chinese.

We were forced to hire the bumi putra graduates so as to have the right mixture and later on I had a lot to do with hiring more of these people, going around to the different universities in different parts of the country.

While we were there, Kuala Lumpur had a population of maybe a million and a half. Now it is a city of several million. It has some huge buildings now, including some of the tallest in the world – like the Petronas twin towers.

Petronas was the government oil company and we were just contractors to Petronas. This meant we had to show them what we were doing. They had to OK everything we did, including drilling programs, shipping, etc. Everything had to be explained to them and that was part of my job. Sometimes they were not happy with what we were planning to do and balked at some of our projects. As Chief Interpreter I would go over and explain to them why we were doing this or that.

The "bright spot effect" I talked about earlier was very prominent in that basin. There was a lot of gas and low percentage gas in the fluids. You could have drilling on the low area in the structure in time but, when you included the velocity differences between the off and on, you were actually drilling on the high. This was difficult for these young, inexperienced geophysicists to understand. Helping them was a good part of my job alongside helping to direct the seismic programs, the geophysical work and then doing the evaluation of that work.

The bright spots were very prominent in several of the fields I worked over. You could pinpoint the end of these sand bodies as they went from gas-filled sand to water-filled sand or pinchout of the sand body. This way you could plan your development wells on these bright spots. It was very interesting work.

I was the senior man at that stage and I knew the exploration manager quite well. He knew I had been around a bit so I was used in other ways, too. I made several reports on the bright spot technology. Another task had to do with dealing with the local fishermen who were affected by our work.

The fishermen had to be involved in planning our off-shore geophysical work. In the East China Sea where we had our big concession (the north half of the eastern off-shore Malaysian peninsula) we had done some earlier mini-type geophysical work off-shore before the concessions were awarded. Based on those data we applied for all the Malaysian acreage in the East China Sea Basin. As it happened, they wouldn't give us all the off-shore on that east side – only half of it. But they said, "Which do you want – the north half or the south half?" Well, the data we had was only shallow penetration so we decided that the north half was the one we wanted and we got that. It extended two degrees north to five degrees north or something like that – very near the equator. It turned out that the north did have most of the hydrocarbons. There were both gas and oil in the East China Sea Basin as it became commonly known later.

There were lots of fishermen working in all those waters. The way they operated was to lower wire pots just as we do for lobster. Theirs were a little bigger with an opening and a cord between the pot and the surface. There would be a float at the surface and a little marker. Every week or two they would pull up these pots, take out the fish and then drop the pots down again. But when we went to do our off-shore seismic work, we needed to drag our cables just below the surface which helped keep them quieter. If you dragged them on the surface you got a lot of noise from the waves and the sound of the boat. But when you did this and then made turns and circles in your seismic program you would collect these baskets and their extensions and floats. There they would be on your cable creating all kinds of noise. So the data we had acquired in some of the areas with this shallow-type streamer was pretty poor data. One solution was to remove these baskets and extensions from the area and put them somewhere else for use later. The exploration manager gave me the job of going out and negotiating with these fisherman as to how much we would pay them for moving their baskets to another location.

I did this for several years – from 1975 to 1979. I'd go out to the east coast and the government fisheries man would get the fishermen to come into a central location where I would meet them. We would discuss the problems and the areas we wanted to work in. Of course the areas we wanted to work in were all over our concession. Giving plots and directions to the fishermen was a little different from what we are used to doing. Explaining all this to them – what we wanted to do, and in what direction – could be a problem. Of course, the big issue for them was money. How many baskets did they have, how much would they get per basket, and so on. Eventually, I would come to an agreement with them. I'd take money that I got from the comptroller back in KL with me and divvy it out. It would be counted several times. They'd watch the count, then count it again, and finally be happy.

This didn't always go over very well back at the comptroller's office. "What is Hajash doing with all that money?" Of course, I accounted for it all with my exploration manager and he was very happy with the arrangement. Eventually, however, we had to decide on the

146

number of baskets and price for each guy and pay them later by cheque. It was fun negotiating with them. When we were finished, usually later in the morning, we'd have a big lunch. It was usually fish, lots of fish.

I also looked after the importing of equipment. We had contractors to do the survey work and they had to bring their equipment into the area. We had another concession in north Borneo of Sabah which is still one of the Malaysian Federation of States. We had a little problem there trying to get the contractor's equipment in. The authorities were holding it up and we couldn't do our survey. The exploration manager sent me over there to talk to them. We talked it all over and came to an agreement. I did a lot of work accounting for all the equipment that could be brought in but, in a day or two, we had that done. I had a little bit of free time after that. I got to know some of the helicopter pilots there and one of them said, "Hey, you aren't doing anything. Come and help me." So I said I would. He was taking barrels of petroleum out to remote locations where we were setting up navigating bases for the seismic service. We took off with the barrels tied to these rubber floats on the helicopter. When we reached the location he said, "I can't set this thing down on that." There were sharp sticks and crud all over the area. So he said, "I've got an axe here – why don't you get out on the float. I'll hover as low as I can and you get off. I'll hover above you until you get this crud cleared up and then I can land." So I got out and stood on this darn thing, holding the axe, until we got down low. I jumped off. He moved away while I cleared an area then down he came and we tried to unload this drum. Unfortunately, there was a steep grade to the area he had chosen. When we unloaded the drum, it rolled down and finally stopped in the brush. Later on I heard the guys had to go down there with jerry cans and bring the stuff back up, cursing the chopper guy. It was quite an interesting outing.

Then it was back to Malaysia and normal work. We had a small field in Sabah called Tembungo. The geology there was different from the east coast geology. It was more highly faulted and quite tricky but we produced oil from the field there for several years.

We failed to have the contract signed with the government but we were getting ready to put in some platforms for off-shore production. The Company, however, decided to shut down all the production-type work while the negotiations were still going on. We stopped work on the platforms. The negotiations were quite acrimonious at times – somewhat like the ones back in Baghdad. Our manager was a big Texas oil man who had worked in Libya before. He was rather overbearing in manner and I don't think that went down too well with the chief negotiator for Petronas – who was a little guy about five foot four. Anyway, we were thinking of moving out of there and getting our data down to Singapore. Safety of the data was of utmost importance. We were afraid they might just come in and take the data away from us but, after about a year, an agreement was reached and the first platform was finished off.

Something odd happened with that. They had decided they would put the platform in a certain place and this meant in a certain depth of water. The water depth varied from zero to 250 feet in the deepest part of the eastern off-shore and you had to build the proper length "leg" for the rig. I remember they decided to move the first platform from where they had intended to place it to another location. This meant they had to chop off thirty feet of leg – a little complication there. Anyway, we got things going again and put in platforms. I think the first one was put in in 1975 – maybe even '76 – and now I don't know how many there are there. I left at the end of March, 1980, and we had found several more oil and gas fields.

I'll bet the producing oil and gas fields number in the thirties now. We used to load the oil off-shore from some big loading platforms. I remember their engineering was quite unlike that used in other places. I don't know how they are doing it now. I know they have built some pipelines to shore for the gas. Some of it is being used by Malaysian industry and perhaps some is being exported. I've lost touch. I left in March of 1980 – that's more than 26 years ago now. I'm sure much has happened. That basin was very prolific. There were no gigantic oil and gas fields but they were all economic and certain to be a real boon to the Malaysian economy.

There were other major industries in Malaysia, of course. One was rubber. They had rubber trees by the millions – many rubber plantations throughout the country. There had been a lot of British planters out there and when we got there a few were still left. At the military golf course where I played there were rubber trees and there was a shy little Chinese fellow who came out to tap the trees and take the "sap" away. He'd peek out from behind the trees and watch us playing golf, and we'd peek back at him doing his work.

Soon after we got there things started changing. I guess rubber wasn't as valuable anymore because we were making tires and other products from petroleum sources instead of from rubber sap. For whatever reason, they decided to switch to growing palm nut to make palm oil. They'd tear out these rubber trees and plant these beautiful little palm trees. In a very short time – four to five years – they would harvest the palm nuts and extract the oil. I remember one of the problems with those trees was the rats. The trees were quite a low-growing species and the rats

149

would climb up them and eat the nuts – like the gophers in western Canada and the birds that used to eat our grain. So they brought in cobras. The cobras would catch the rats and this kept the rat population down. Anyway, changing from rubber to palm oil was the big thing in the days we were there. Now I think palm oil has lost favour because of the new awareness of cholesterol and other health concerns. Never mind, they've got lots of oil and gas to keep them going!

Figure 15: Armed Forces Golf Club, Kuala Lumpur.

Chapter 9 – A Final Posting in the UK

From Malaysia Mickey and Donna moved to England again where they spent the last six years of Mickey's more than four decades with the Esso-Exxon group of companies, from April, 1980, until he retired in August, 1986, the last year working as an Exploration Scientist.

In 1980 here we were again, back in England. As soon as I arrived at the office I immediately started doing interpretation work. At the same time I was looking for a house to buy. I was staying not too far away where I could walk to work from the temporary lodgings.

I expected that this would be my last assignment. I had been promised that it would be a senior position. I'd be asked to do various assignments – evaluate various areas. When I got there I found I was working for a manager I had been acquainted with when I was in the New York and Houston offices. At that time I had been working for the regional overall management doing their bidding and carrying out their wishes. I would relay their ideas and mine, of course, to the area exploration managers. Unfortunately, these suggestions from the central office had created a bit of friction with this particular manager I was now supposed to work with. He was a real know-it-all. He would always interject his opinions. We wouldn't have the right answer – he had the answer, and he knew all about it. He carried this to an extreme. For example, during lunch hour he would come along and we'd start a discussion of something, not necessarily having to do with work. He would interrupt and say, "No, no, that wasn't the way it went," and carry this on through the entire lunch hour. It got to the point where we would try to sneak out for lunch and hope he didn't see us and come along with us. We sure didn't invite him.

Anyway, that was the kind of manager he was. He wanted to do everything himself. He'd edit every letter that came out of the office. So I knew this was coming. I dug in with my usual work ethic and tried to do the best I could. When my wife joined me we were still staying at the small hotel I had put up in. I kept going to the office, walking there and back. In the evenings I was pretty beat. I had to work hard at the office and on a kind of table that I was not used to. I had been used to a flat table top, not a drafting table. This meant I was using muscles I had never used before, reaching and bending, so I was pretty pooped when I got home. But Donna was there and we'd usually watch television. They had two channels then. I remember once they had the world snooker championships on. One of the players was Cliff Thorburn. So I'd watch that most evenings as my entertainment. I remember seeing him win this world championship and when he shot that perfect game – that would be 147. I remember watching all the way through. The TV coverage was very good. It provided a nice break in the routine.

We finally found a house and got moved in. There were all the usual problems fixing things. Donna always puts her mark on things so we had to do it to her high standards. It was a very nice house and we enjoyed living in it for over five years.

There were many geophysicists and geologists in the big new office the Company had there, right in the town of Esher, which is southwest of London near the new A3. The fourth floor was a large room where we had our big meetings, taught our training courses, held ethics sessions and the like. Across the street was Sandown Racetrack. You could see some of the races going on from the fourth floor windows. I remember one day we were looking out and saw a big commotion on the far side with ambulances arriving and so on. It turned out Prince Charles had fallen off his horse and broken his shoulder.

The technical work itself usually involved evaluating acreage that came up for sale. There were probably two or three sales while I was there. That was hard work in that you had to put in extra time. I had other projects I worked on besides evaluation of all the other geophysical work.

I was also in charge of recruiting geophysicists for our office. One or two of us would set up dates at the universities and interview prospective geophysicists. It was interesting, fun, different, especially seeing how the English universities compared to the universities back here. We visited Cambridge a couple of times. Redding was a favourite place because they had a good geology school there. We would also go north up to places like Leeds. We visited Glasgow once or twice and Edinburgh as well as Aberdeen. So we got to know a fair amount of the country and the teaching staffs at the universities. We did hire quite a few of the kids – probably two or three a year. Over the six years we ended up hiring mostly UK geophysicists and geologists. We also got over to Ireland where we visited Dublin and Galway. We didn't go into Northern Ireland because of the problems there. Instead, we had the applicants from there come down to Dublin. We hired kids from pretty well all the universities we visited. To make the final choices we'd have them come down to Esher where we would interview them again and introduce them to the office and the managers. The committee and I would finally make a choice from those we had interviewed and we'd propose this candidate to the manager.

We had charge of the North Sea and onshore UK but I also got to see some of the operations elsewhere in Europe. We had production acreages in various African countries as well. I remember going to the Ivory Coast and looking over their data. They had made some minor discovery and I was asked to go out there and help them evaluate the data, advise on the geophysics part of it and suggest how to carry on from there to develop that oil field. I spent over a week there.

I made a couple of trips to the Research Centre, of course, as we had to keep up to date with the current state of the art of our geophysics and exploration in general.

I was involved in the evaluation of all the geophysicists in the UK office. I had a chief geophysicist above me and I was the Chief Interpreter. This Chief Geophysicist was known to be not much of a technical man and I guess he got his promotions through his good looks and manner. Besides that, he was losing his memory. He was probably 45 years of age. I don't know what it was – early Alzheimer's or what – but he was definitely losing it. When the manager finally realized what was happening, I think in the end he was glad to have me there to bear the brunt of all the technical stuff and even the personnel evaluations.

The Chief Geophysicist's memory was so bad it was hard to believe. I had my 40th anniversary with Esso Companies while I was there so they had a big to-do over it. There hadn't been many people with them that long even then (and few even now). I was allowed to invite three or four for this luncheon – the manager and the geophysicists. It was all very nice. I forget what I got – a wristwatch, or whatever, and a pin. I still have my pin. It has four diamonds, one for each ten years of service. Anyway, about two weeks after the luncheon, the geophysicist called me and said, "Hey, I see your fortieth anniversary is coming up – I think we'd better have a party." God, I just couldn't believe it, even though I knew he was very forgetful. I mean, he'd been there, helped plan it, helped decide who was to come, and so on. But he just completely forgot it. That was typical of his abilities at the time.

Well, that's the way it was and promotions remained a problem. I had been promoted slowly at times and faster at other times. I think the fastest promotion had been with the Iraq Petroleum Company. When I joined them in Baghdad I'm sure I was over-qualified for the job, but within a year of my being there I think they realized they had somebody who could do them some good. I remember the first year there they reviewed my salary and gave me what amounted to a twenty-five per cent increase. That was unheard of – back in Imperial, for sure. There were other times, too, when I made good progress. In Malaysia Jack Armitage took good care of all his employees, including me. Of course, at times when the oil business was booming and everybody was hiring, help would be scarce and they would rush around and give you more money to make sure you didn't leave to go to other companies. But at times I thought my promotions through the Imperial Esso Company were slower than they should have been. Maybe we all think that way. I didn't let this affect my work, however. I had a strong work ethic and carried on because that was the thing to do. When I was getting near the end, I was hoping to get promoted so I could retire well. Another consideration was that if you reached a certain level in the hierarchy you could take all your pension money in a lump sum instead of having it doled out monthly. I knew some of the upper managers were able to do this so I was hoping that one day I would get up to that level because I thought that was the best way to go.

I also knew while I was in the UK under this particular manager my prospects were poor because of the friction I referred to earlier. Because of this I worried I wouldn't get up there. My last promotion had been in 1979 through Jack Armitage. Now it was getting up to '85 and there was no promotion and only modest increases at the level I was at. To make matters worse, of course, my Chief Geophysicist was losing his marbles. The manager was worried about it but couldn't replace him immediately, I guess.

Under these circumstances, I was about ready to leave in 1985. When they came to me and said, "We'd like you to stay another year or so," my reply was "Well, I don't know about that – I'm ready to go and you fellows haven't been very nice to me here lately." They came back with, "Oh no, please stay, we'll try and fix up whatever needs to be done." Lo and behold, they gave me that last final promotion which took me up to the level where I could take out my pension as a lump sum. That happened in May of 1985 and I was quite pleased with that. Way back when I started, salaries had been really low. The increase with that promotion in 1985 was five and a half times my yearly salary to start, and that doesn't take into consideration the exchange value of the money. This raise was in American dollars. Because the US dollar was so much higher than the Canadian then, the real increase was fantastic. What made it even better was that our pension at that time was based on the average of your last three years. I spent another sixteen months after that with the Company so my three-year average was really very good.

During that last year I was winding down but still carrying on – evaluating acreages and helping the geophysicists in their work. I still found the work interesting and I was enjoying it very much. Then, getting near the end in 1986 a little slump came along. Whereas 1984 and '85 had been a big high, things slumped in '86 and we went into one of those cyclic downturns when the Company would ask some of the people to leave – mainly from the lower ranks, but others too. They offered a package to encourage them to go. It was a modest one – not as good as some of the others they had offered when they wanted to get rid of a bunch of employees during earlier slumps – but, by this time, I was ready to go – so I went to my boss and said, "Put me at the top of the list." That happened the end of August, 1986, after 40 years and 6 months of most enjoyable work.

My pension also benefited from the benefits the Company had provided for being overseas so many years. When you were overseas, especially in the first few years, they gave you a bonus of 1 extra year for every two years you had spent overseas for pension consideration. (They changed that later on in 1972 to one extra year's credit for every four years spent overseas and I believe they've now done away with that altogether.) In addition to this bonus pension credit for overseas work, they were quite liberal in their living allowances and other extra allowances. This meant that my tax situation was probably better than it would have been if I had remained with the Company back home.

It was then a matter of doing things to wind up my career with Imperial Oil, Standard Oil of New Jersey and Exxon Esso after forty and a half years. That entailed traveling to New York to be drummed out and advised as to what they'd do, how things would go, and to get my input into all of this. I had a couple of days in New York and then I went back home to organize the move. All that went very smoothly. The Company was very liberal and generous in their help in getting me retired and moved, but getting the money back to Canada was tricky. With the whole amount of my pension involved, I wanted to get it back to Canada without paying any extraordinary amount of tax. I'd already paid US tax on the retirement sum and I didn't want to pay some more when bringing it into Canada. I found out from other people in the Company how best to do this. This entailed getting all the money stashed somewhere outside the country and sending it into Canada before we got home. If you brought it in after you were in Canada, you were liable for tax on it.

I spent quite a bit of time getting all the money over to a bank in the Jersey Isles. The idea was to then transfer it to our bank in Victoria. I split the whole amount in half and put one half in Donna's account and the other half in mine. That worked out pretty well, but when I got home I discovered that one of the big chunks had been put in Donna's bank alright but it had then been yanked out and kept some place for sixteen days before being put back in again. So I went to talk to the bank about this. They didn't have much of an answer and they didn't do very much to recompense us for the interest we had lost. I suspect they had been in trouble for laundering offshore money in some instance and they were getting leery about large sums of money coming from the Jersey Isles. But that was the only such instance.

Another twist relating to our finances was this: I had a bunch of Exxon shares accumulated through my Thrift Plan. The Company was quite liberal in encouraging employees to participate in their Thrift Plan and I had purchased shares all the way along. After getting some advice, I took all my shares to England and sold them there at the going price. There was no tax to pay there. We also sold the house in England for £255,000. We had bought it for £115,000 so there was a big gain there – and no tax on that either. Overall, I avoided paying tax on my retirement assets pretty well.

Chapter 10 – Retirement in Victoria

In the fall of 1986, after Mickey had spent over forty years with the Esso-Exxon group of companies, Mickey and Donna retired to Victoria, British Columbia.

I retired on November 16th, 1986, and went to Victoria. There were just the two of us and our third or fourth Yorkie. The dog actually got through Customs before we did and was waiting for us. We were held up because of all the furniture we had – we had accumulated a lot of antiques along the way. We had to list all the pieces and put an evaluation on them all. If they were over 100 years old or if you had owned them for a certain length of time they could be brought in duty-free. We got by without paying duty on just about everything. They questioned the odd thing like carved ivory. How do you prove how old that is? The elephant was pretty old before they took the tusk from him but it is hard to tell how old the carving is. The new looks like the old and the old looks like the new. As I say, we got all our stuff in alright but, of course, we didn't have a house to put it in so we had to store all this stuff in Vancouver where we stayed with our daughter for two months. We then came over to Victoria and looked for a place. Without much ado, the first house we looked at, Donna stepped inside the door and said, "You're buying this, this is my house." So I couldn't do anything. I couldn't dicker. I just smiled and paid the price and there we were. I think it was listed at $395,000 and we offered that and got the house that afternoon.

So that was all there was to the house shopping here. We're still in that house. I'm sitting right here, doing this dictation in it, and we've enjoyed every minute of it. And that is another story – from '86 to '06 now, another 20 years.

We moved in January fifteenth and got our furniture out of storage in Vancouver. We also had a bunch of furniture left in Houston in 1974 that we hadn't taken to Singapore and Kuala Lumpur. We got that to Victoria later (after 12 years) in various states of repair. Of course, we had to get all that stuff fixed up and set up in the house. That took quite some time and doing. Donna spent a lot of time finding places to get these things repaired. For one display cupboard we finally had to get some moulded glass from San Francisco. They made us a curbed moulding. All that took part of a year and finally, on January 15, 1988, we had a house-warming party and invited all our friends from around Victoria to come and visit us. I remember that even then we didn't have everything shipshape and had to put up a few card tables. We had a good house warming. One incident I remember: We had people coming from Vancouver and on late Friday they were coming in on the highway after leaving the ferry. Coming by Elk Lake they saw some to-do going on which turned out to be the tragic capsize of the rowers from UVic and the subsequent death of two young men.

We then settled down and bought our cars. First I bought a big Chevrolet demo, which lasted me a good while – well over 10 years. I handed it down to our daughter and it disintegrated after that. Donna got a new Toyota Camry that lasted more than 10 years. Then she got a new 1997 BMW 328, I think it was. I got me a used Olds 95 which I still have. So we had the cars and the house all fixed up. What else to do?

I had to get the yard in shape so I worked on that and played some golf. I joined the Royal Colwood Club and played there two or three times a week. And we had children nearby. Our daughter was divorced by then and had moved

160

from Vancouver to Victoria. We bought her a house. Our son was in Vancouver and we helped him buy a house there and later supported them both somewhat – mainly my daughter.

Then, of course, there was my daughter's yard. She had a yard of trees, which she had had cut down and there they were in odd lengths – stumps all over. I went over, piled up the logs, split the wood and started removing huge roots. Of course they were tough. I used an axe and a crowbar on them but without much success. I had all kinds of suggestions about how to get the roots out and none worked. I had a big drill with a three-quarter-inch bit and I drilled holes in all of these stumps and poured gunk into them (I don't remember what it was) and then waited. Well, that didn't do much. I left them six to eight months, but got tired of waiting and started digging them out manually. Well, that didn't work too well, either, so I got a burn permit and made little fires with all the crud I had collected around by each root. This did a fair job on a lot of them but I still had to dig around them, one piece after another, to get the stumps out. After that, it was a matter of cleaning up the yard and leveling it. Of course it was all weedy so I got a shovel and spade and dug up the whole yard, shovel by shovel. I dug out all the weeds and piled them up in one huge pile. Of course, you couldn't burn them so we had them hauled away – a big truckload. Finally, I got the yard all dug and I leveled it by pulling a ladder I had with weights on it – pulling it round and round. Then we got in a couple of loads of topsoil and I spread all that by hand and leveled it again, got grass seed, seeded it, raked it in, watered it and it grew. It was a reasonable lawn. Of course, with the young kids tearing around, it wasn't too well looked after and the cutting wasn't always done – it was very haphazard. Anyway, I did all that by hand. That took me about two summers. Mind you, I didn't work every day or all day, but my routine would be to be there by 7:30 or 8 and work till noon. Then I'd either take the rest of the day off or, on golf days, I'd try to golf. None of this helped my handicap very much.

At home in our place there were lots of trees, mainly oak, but around the perimeter there were cedars. We had about three-quarters of an acre of garden surrounded by these pyramid cedars which grew like Topsy. The front had a five and a half foot high hedge so about half the yard was hedge and two-thirds was cedars. The Gary oaks were in various states of disrepair. I had a good gardener at that time and he could climb and cut trees. Whenever we had a problem with one we'd get a permit from the municipality and away he'd go and top them. He did a good job. He didn't just lop the top off but would drop it piece by piece and that would do the least damage to the lawn. Then he would cut it up and split it and I'd haul it in a wheelbarrow down into the basement and stack the wood there. Every oak that we cut – about ten of them in nineteen years – I've hauled into the basement to burn in the fireplace. I'd even pick up the stuff that fell off in the storms and put it down there to use for burning. No open-air burning is allowed anywhere here now. The first few years I did a bit, but only on certain days. Now there's no burning.

Anyway, that happened in the early years. Now we keep working on the gardens. I still cut the grass myself and have done so for nineteen years. We make compost in two big bins and use it on the rest of the garden and the trees.

After that, of course, what do we do in the winter? People usually go somewhere for a few weeks or months but we went on golf trips, mainly down to the States, and we'd play several tournaments with the Geophysicists' Golf Tourney – the Doodlebug. We used to have our annual tournament in

Banff. It still goes on, but now the old guys from here and Calgary and a few other places have started the Seismic Senior Tourney. At first it was held somewhere in the San Diego area. One year we went to Whitefish, Montana, but by that time the exchange rate was high and we said, "Why not just do our thing in Canada?" We started playing in the interior of BC. One place was in the Castlegar area where we played three golf courses in three days. That went on until just about three years ago. Now we old seniors – the original gang – don't go anymore. But that was a lot of fun, meeting old friends again, socializing, playing golf. After all the traveling we did with the Company from 1960 on, I was rather glad to just relax at home – if working in my daughter's garden was relaxing.

We did make a few other trips – to the UK and to Portugal. Friends of ours from Springfield, Missouri, had a Portuguese maid for years. This maid traveled all over with them – they went a lot of places. In her later years of service, they set her up in an apartment in Portugal which she furnished, and it served as a sort of base for people who wanted to visit Portugal and her hometown. We did that a couple of times. My wife and daughter also visited there on their own.

We also took a long cruise one year starting in Houston (Galveston), across the Atlantic to Cadiz, into the Mediterranean visiting Malta, Sicily and Athens. I forget the name of the ship. It wasn't too big. We had about six hundred people on board, most of them from Victoria. It was a lot of fun. From Athens we went to England where we visited a bit, then came home. We all had the various ailments that you get with trips of this kind. I'm not much of a sailor, but I enjoyed that one.

In addition to all this, we have other activities which keep us occupied. Golf – that's a lifetime thing – and when you retire you have more time to play. In the early days, when we were just starting our careers, we had very little time for golf and it was only a few years after, when you had the odd buck and the family was starting to grow a little bit, that you played and tried to learn this very difficult game. I did that intermittently through the years. Playing all over the world, as we were able to do, made it very, very interesting. We played a number of golf courses in the Malaysia area from Singapore up to Thailand. In Malaysia, where I was a Royal member, we played every weekend. There was very little gardening to do there so we had pretty well all of Saturday and Sunday to golf.

In addition to golf here in Victoria, I joined the Rotary Club in 1996 at the invitation of my very good friend, Maury VanVliet. I've participated in their activities and their charity work and am now the chairman of their Community Needs Committee.

We have a number of other charities we give to. Between 2000 and 2003 we gave two endowments to the United Way and to our Foundation. We give $75 thousand to each. In all those four years we averaged about $62 thousand of tax-deductible earnings to charities including the Foundation. If you add the Foundation's donations of roughly $38 thousand per year, during those four years it comes out to about 100 thousand dollars each year that we have given to charities, either privately or out of the Foundation. Besides that, I have volunteered my time for many other things and especially to the United Way. I've been with them for nineteen years now. It's almost a year-round commitment, especially working with the leadership group where we work on our plans, nurture our clients and canvass for seven months. There are, of course, other things a retired person

164

can do. We joined the Esso Annuitant Group for all the Esso retirees. The Company offers fifty dollars per person for the group to do with what they want. I've participated in that as vice-president, president, and past president – which is a three-year commitment. As well, I have started up an Esso United Way Campaign and we canvass our own Esso annuitants. They are all very good. Our Vancouver Island group have been the leading Esso givers in Canada per person. We are quite proud of that.

Mentioning other charities, while we were still overseas, we had managed to invest in some property in Esquimalt, eventually acquiring a whole block frontage – old residential properties and a corner store. It was getting to be a burden to keep it up because the buildings were old and starting to fall apart. We finally sold the whole block frontage to a senior citizens' housing society who have many buildings for the needy in Victoria. They purchased it through government funds and built a beautiful fifty-two-apartment, five and a half floors complex. It was the first building in Esquimalt that was higher than three storeys. That was because it was a seniors' assisted living facility and the authorities allowed it to be built to this height. We were proud to be part of that and attended the opening. We actually got Imperial Oil to donate a little money to the project. We also donated some money and Donna gave them a painting for their game room upstairs.

Charities and donations: Here's a typical list from 2003: We made a donation to the Foundation, with an insurance policy to benefit the United Way when the second of us passes away of $125,000. We also donated to the following: Mustard Seed, War Amps, Victoria Hospice, Hospital Foundation, Liver Association, Remembrance Day, Firefighters Burn foundation, Oak Bay Rescue, Heart and Stroke Foundation, Canadian Association for the Blind,

Child Rescue, Salvation Army, Rotary Club, Single Parents Association, Canadian Cancer Society, Canadian Diabetes Society, the University of Alberta. We also give an average of 14 scholarships per year at $2500 each.

I've also continued to be involved in sports activities in some way or another. We have a big golf tournament here every year. It alternates between the different golf courses and ours is included so I volunteer to help with that every time. But I also worked in the Ladies' Tournament, the BC Summer Games twice, and I worked in the fastball tournament one year. I kept volunteering. Then came the 1994 Commonwealth Games. Of course, I volunteered – this time as a team attaché. That was something I could do. After traveling all over the world and with teams coming from all over the world, it seemed natural. I didn't apply for any specific team. I could have asked for the Malaysian team, I suppose, but I didn't. I just put in my name and they gave me the Sierra Leone team. I didn't know a thing about them or the problems they were going through. Anyway, I was their team attaché and got organized for their arrival and all that business. It was quite a story.

I met the team and got them shepherded into residence at the University. After a certain time, the teams were to come for the raising of the flag and that kind of business. I arranged for our team to come out at such and such a time for the ceremony and to meet the other officials.

Well, the time came, and no team. I got to a 'phone and, nope, they weren't going to come. They didn't have any clothes, their country wasn't supporting them so they weren't going to come out to this flag-raising. God! I rushed over there and begged and pleaded with them. I said, "Come on, guys, get with it." Finally we got the manager and a few others to come out. But the manager couldn't force the rest of them. He was a really nice guy. He was the son of the first Governor General of Sierra Leone when they took over from the British.

Well, that was the start of it. They didn't have any presentable team clothes, no athletic clothes or running shoes, no warm-up suits, no money, no nothing. Even the manager didn't have much. I know I helped him get his own clothes. We went to Sears and got him some stuff. We tried to organize clothes for the rest of the team from different places and we had some success. The Rotary Club pitched in. I wasn't a member at the time, but friends of mine realized the problem we had and gave us $1000 to buy shoes and equipment. It was a team of about twelve, so $1000 could buy quite a few shoes. We went to Team Sales and they contributed track wear. The Bay contributed team clothes like white shirts, pants, and jackets. Of course, this got into the press, the Times Colonist, and people wanted to help so we let it be known they could donate to the Sierra Leone team at such and such a number and address (our home address). So Donna and Gwen McLaws, I remember, became involved in receiving and recording these monies, manning the phone and keeping track of the donations. They used this money to buy equipment and I recall jackets were part of that.

This was a big help. But these fellows still had a grudge. For example, during the opening ceremonies, with the athletes filing in and all, guess what? Not a one of mine showed up. Just the manager. He was the only guy who showed up. I had wanted to be with the team but I guess the CBC didn't like our combination of colours in our team attaché uniforms – which clashed some way with their TV presentation so the team attachés were not allowed to walk with their team. So there was the team manager – by himself. At that time he didn't have these clothes we got for him later. He was just in his ordinary clothes with a baseball cap on. But he carried the flag. I was there and I was just a little mortified.

They did, however, individually participate in their events along the way. One of them, the 100-meter guy, had been training in Florida at some small school. He'd been sent over there a year before. He was a good athlete – very outgoing – and he fought his way through the preliminaries and got to the finals. He was in the pack until about 10 meters from the end and, boy, he just dug his way out of that and ended up getting second place. So that was the big silver. Then the relay team he anchored qualified for the finals on Sunday. This was on the Saturday of the last week. We set up a big party for them here at our house with friends and guests and the whole team. There was a TV group here from Channel Six which set up downstairs. I have a big games room down there and they took yards of film, talked to the guys and got the silver medal winner on tape. It was quite a nice day at the end of August so a lot of folks were outside on the patio. The boys behaved pretty well, ate the food we had (lots of fruit for them – a big part of their diet) and drank a lot of juice. They didn't goof off on alcohol or anything.

However, the games authorities had done testing on all the athletes and had gotten an A sample from our silver medal guy. I didn't know there was any problem, but then they did the B sample and it tested positive. I guess the manager must have been alerted after the A sample which came late Saturday. So the silver medal guy was disqualified and his medal taken away. The relay team was also disqualified.

So there was disappointment at the end. The poor fellow at the centre of it all was devastated and he didn't go back to

Sierra Leone but stayed in the States, I think. The papers never did report where he ended up. Quite a story, eh?

Figure 16: Jack Armitage, J.B. Benka-Coker (Manager of the Sierra Leone Team), and Mickey at the Commonwealth Games, Victoria, 1994.

Chapter 11 – Epilogue

In this concluding chapter, Mickey speaks of friends, family and health.

People

I'd like to talk about some people, friends and relatives. Start out with Dad. It was he who decided Hungary wasn't the future for his family. His father was the mayor of Matramindszent and had been for many years and Dad was not going to be the next one. I think Dad wanted to have something better for his family and I'm glad that he did so. As I have recounted earlier, he went out on his own to Estevan, Saskatchewan, and worked like a dog to earn enough money to bring us out in two years' time. Later on, when things seemed hopeless and terrible with the depression and with no jobs for a fairly new immigrant, with the kids growing up and the boys – myself included – getting into trouble because there was not much to do there, he decided we should move somewhere else so he and the older boys could get work. That's when we moved to the Brooks area to try to get us a better life. I admired Dad for those kinds of decisions and Mom for being there in the background quietly supporting us. She often spoke up for us when we were having problems with Dad. As the boys got older and wanted to be involved in the decisions on the farm, they and Dad had different ideas and had lots of disagreements.

I also owe my brothers a lot. When my Dad wasn't around they kept me straight – they were my caretakers. Then I owed them for sacrificing so much without realizing it, for going to work so early – Joe when he was fifteen and Jim at thirteen. They were working for the family and I got the benefit of their work and sacrifice. I started school in Estevan and got to grade five there. The teachers involved got me interested in books and reading. I would read anything I could get my hands on, especially the history of Canada and the early traders.

I might say something here about my feelings concerning Canada and being Canadian. Our whole family – and I perhaps more than anybody else in the family – am a Canadian first and foremost. I maintain my Hungarian language a bit and some Hungarian memories. Through visits back over the years I've maintained some acquaintance with what's going on there. But I am a Canadian and I hate to see others coming here and behaving the way they behaved back home. I get pretty upset with all those people – I think the Canadian laws and immigration should be such that those kinds of people should be sent back home. I feel strongly about that. For instance, when I used to play football, especially at university, but also with Calgary, before the game they'd sing or play "O Canada". We would stand there whatever the weather and I became emotional when that was played. I think that was the most emotion I've ever had.

Back to Brooks. Our landlord, Mr. Taylor from Seattle, was a wonderful man. I was a shy young kid and he helped bring me out of my shell a little bit. He was only there a month a year during hunting season. The one suit I had to go off to university with was given to me by him. He also later helped the family by selling the land to them at practically the same price he had purchased it for ten years earlier. Others in Brooks who had a big influence on my life included my teacher, Mr. Fia, who was the Assistant Principal in the high school there. He was a fairly young fellow then. He was the track, hockey and basketball coach who often played with us as the fifth member of the team. He moved my career along athletically. He eventually went off to the Army where he served in the artillery. When he came back, he stopped off in Winnipeg and began working in the peacetime rocketry industry. He became the leading rocketry man in Canada ("The Father of Canadian Rocketry") and was honoured for that. I remember at the junior track meet in Calgary I was the leading junior athlete there. He was there to hold my hand and he encouraged me.

In Brooks there were the Ingrams – Oliver and Doug – local merchants where we did our shopping. They were helpful in getting me the scholarship to Oklahoma (the scholarship I couldn't take up because of the wartime restrictions on travel to the States). A lawyer, Mr. De LaVergne, and the train agent, Mr. Crook, were also helpful. While I was at university, the people involved in Calgary junior football were all helpful – they even let me carry the ball (the first time I had carried the ball) as their fullback. In baseball the Purity 99 team welcomed me with open arms and let me get out there and do my stuff. I had two summers with them.

At university Maury VanVliet was very influential in my life. He was the football coach and mentor in the two years – junior and senior. When I was president of the Men's Athletic Board he would be at the meetings, guiding me and teaching me how to do things at the committee level. Percy Daggle was his assistant and he was a very likeable, nice fellow. Classmates in the last year of mining were very helpful getting me through that year and my professors in mining were very supportive. Mr. Lilge was very friendly and supportive – I remember him especially because he gave me a mark of 100 in "Fire Assaying." That was the best mark I ever had in university – some of the others weren't that great. My classmate, Malcolm Clark, who helped me make contact with his Dad, who was the head of mining engineering, and my DU brothers were all helpful to a young country kid coming straight from the farm to university. I needed a lot of help and a lot of tutoring. Jack Jorgens, who was a couple of years ahead of me, was one of the most helpful. I met him later in life after a gap of fifty years. He was quite pleased at the way I had grown up since he was the one who had got me going in university. He had helped me prepare for the talks and speeches I'd have to give to get elected. Andy Andrekson, one of the fellows I met there, became a lifetime friend. He was a very kind man – we would talk for hours. Margaret Weir, the girl he married, had been a friend of Donna's for years, so we were quite a foursome. (They became acquainted at our wedding – Andy was my best man.)

Now for some people I met at work. Frank Spagins was my first party chief. I met him in Brooks in 1941. He worked hard and was a nice boss, the kind who would never ask you to do anything he wouldn't do himself. He was a very, very nice man, an electrical engineer from Rice University who eventually became the president of Syncrude. He took them through the first tough years. Harold Stoneman whom I met in Brooks and his wife, Helen, also became longtime friends of ours. We would visit them in Springfield, Missouri, after they retired. I remember helping them set up their first house there. We drove up from Houston and I spent two days there putting up the curtains Donna had had made for all the windows of this big house. Jack Armstrong was another I met on that crew in Brooks. He was the number two interpreter to Harold Stoneman for whom he worked for many years. I met him again along the way and he finally became president of Imperial Oil. He retired and I see him every year. He is up in Parksville and a member of our Esso Annuitant Group. Don McIvor got to be president of Imperial Oil after Jack. I met him in Calgary when I was down there. He had just started and we both got posted to

Peace River. We went up in his old car. There were four of us with Donna and our dog. Just north of Moranville his car conked out and we hitchhiked back to Moranville where we knew the garage owner, Louis Trembly, a good friend of Donna's dad. He sent someone off to tow the car back. It was a water pump that had gone. Donna and the dog caught the bus to Grande Prairie where her folks were and Don and I waited for the car and carried on up to Peace River where Don and I worked for a few years.

Gerry Rempel and wife, Lois, I met in the 1950s. He was an honours graduate in physics and got to work for Imperial. He was in the data acquisition and supervision part of it and I got to know him very well. In Edmonton we worked together for six years and we have been great friends ever since. The four of us get together quite often to play golf and do golf tournaments together. Buz Crosby was one of my supervisors. I admired him. He let me do my thing and, at that time, my thing was the right thing. Hector Van Buskirk was a former employee of Imperial who worked for twenty-five years in the geophysical business. He retired but worked another fifteen or twenty years for contract geophysical companies. He was a very friendly, likeable man. George Demille was a different kind of geologist with Imperial Oil. He was self-trained and had never got past high school but he got to be the senior geologist in Imperial Oil. He did a lot of the teaching and I learned more geology from George than I did at university. At Iraq Petroleum Company, Dr. Thiebaud, a French/Swiss geologist, was the exploration manager. He worked in the Middle East in those early days, supervising geological field crews in Egypt and elsewhere. He was my boss when I got to be the Chief Geophysicist in Iraq. He was a wonderful person who would let you do your thing and, if you didn't do it right, he let you know about it. I learned from that and he appreciated what I had done and what I was doing for IPC. I still have

174

the letter of recommendation he wrote for me when I left IPC. It was quite a nice letter.

While I was still there, a Yorkshireman, Dunnington, became the chief geologist. He was a fine geologist who knew the geology of the middle East backwards. He knew it better than any other guy ever in the Middle East. He had written one massive paper on Middle East oil and the habitat. It was a thorough study of the subject because our company could get data from a number of sources because of our multi-company organizational structure. He compiled all this material and I encouraged him to write a paper which he presented to the Institute of Petroleum in London of which I was secretary for a while. I think it's still the best paper yet on Middle East oil.

On to Esso Exploration. I had many bosses there. The one who stands out from the bunch is Jack Armitage who was my boss in Malaysia. He was a Canadian I had met in the Regina area when I was there. He was doing the well-siting on a lot of the wells that I had proposed, written up and predicted depths to the various geological horizons. He would follow the drill bit down and analyze the cuttings and, knowing my reputation, he relied on all my depth predictions to alert himself to various formations that were coming up. As he said many times, they came in within a few feet, so he had full confidence in my work. I worked for him for almost six years there. We became good friends and played golf together. We both retired to Victoria and played golf together at Colwood.

After retirement we have met other people – through the Esso Annuitant Group, golf, Rotary, the United Way. We also have many good business associations. Ralston Alexander, a very fine gentleman, has been our lawyer for thirty years now. This past year he was the head of the B.C.

Law society. There is also my good young broker, Paul Sulich, upon whom I rely to take care of my life-long earnings.

I've met my friend Maury VanVliets' son again. I first met him when he was five years old. Now he's finished his schooling, been successful in his lifetime work and he's retired and living next door. I've asked him to be involved in my affairs. He is the executor of our wills, a member of our Foundation and I hope he will take care of us even after we are gone – a friend forever.

Another couple I want to mention is Harvey Hewetson and his wife, Phyllis. I've known Harvey from about 1948 on and worked with him through the 1940's and 50's in western Canada. Then they came over to England and we socialized with them there. Phyllis is dead now but we see Harvey quite a bit. He lives up in Nanaimo where we get together at the Crow and Gate pub and have a good time. Harvey has been a member of our Foundation for the last few years and has contributed some monies to it.

Here in Victoria I've golfed with Earl Mahaffy. I met him back in the Alberta oil scene, then at the Doodlebug golf tournaments and again here at Colwood. I have played golf with him for the past eighteen years in the US and Canada. He's a great organizer. He's been the president of the SEG and ran the Doodlebug tournament one year. Another golfer I met here is Bob Barkley and his wife, Wendy. He's a really wonderful fellow and a good golfer. I've enjoyed his company and our discussions about things. We generally agree on most things. We both want to do the right things for the country, the club, etc.

Two other Calgarians I met years ago were Harry Hobbs and Ken Moore. I first knew them in the last two years of

176

university. Both were good athletes. Harry took commerce and Ken took law. I played football with them and with Andy Andrekson in that fourth year. The four of us used to go out in the evenings a lot. We were good buddies – someone termed us "the four horsemen". I'd run into them now and then but the last time the four of us were together – well, almost four – was at Andy's funeral. Harry and Ken come out to Victoria every winter. We'd get together and reminisce about football and have some good times together here.

I want to mention my niece, Sandra Hajash, who is living in "the bungalow" now. She is the daughter of my middle brother Jim, and we enjoy seeing her when we visit Brooks each year. The bungalow has received an Alberta Heritage designation.

And I'd like to mention Gordon and Gwen McLaws. Gordon was born in Bassano, Alberta, which is about 40 miles from Brooks. We attended the University of Alberta together, and on graduating, went to work for Imperial Oil, Gordon in Comptrollers and me in Exploration. We both retired to Victoria in '86-'87, joined the Royal Colwood Golf course, the Esso Annuitants Club and the University of Alberta Alumni. Donna and Gwen became good friends. We shared a love of sports, partied together, shared mutual friends, and enjoyed each other's company. I remember when the university abandoned its football program, Gordon was involved in the disposition of uniforms and equipment. The Edmonton Eskimos team was about to join the CFL so the U of A's proud Green and Gold was turned over to them and thereafter became the Eskimos' colors. Gordon died in 2003 and was inducted posthumously into the Tennis Hall of Fame the following year. We grieved with Gwen and supported her in her loss.

Health

One thing I haven't mentioned arc the health problems. I think they affect what we do and how we live our lives. Through my life I've had generally good heath, but the latter part has been hindered and affected by heart problems and the high cholesterol our family seems to have. The Hajash family are great cholesterol-builders. My dad died at sixty-four of a heart attack, my second brother at sixty-four – also a heart attack. My eldest brother passed away but he was older – seventy-six. Dad's brother passed away in his fifties – another heart attack. So I knew it could happen to me. And it did. I first learned that I had high cholesterol in the UK. The Company had good medical people there and they had cottoned on to this and I had started changing my diet – but it had built up.

My first heart attack was in 1993. They didn't do much then but put me on medication. The high cholesterol I had known about before and had tried to reduce it with proper diet. Donna has been very good with the menu – no more sausages or that kind of meat. My first heart attack in '93 was a real shocker. I had an angiogram and they thought they could treat my condition with medication. But later that year I had several other little attacks and in November of '94 went into the hospital for open heart surgery. I convalesced for six days and came home after that. Ever since then I've been fairly OK – taking medication and blood thinners. I've had a couple of mini-strokes in the past six months but they can't seem to find the cause of those.

My eyes, of course, have been getting weaker and weaker. Even in my teens and later, my eyesight affected my play, especially in baseball. Even in university nobody ever suggested having my eyes checked. It wasn't until a driving test in Peace River in 1952 that I learned some of my driving problems could be from not having 20/20 vision. I started wearing glasses from then on. I tried contacts in Malaysia but, with the perspiration and dust, they would stick and pop out. It was hard to find them on the green fairways so I packed that in and just wore glasses. I had a cataract operation on my right eye about five years ago, and the other about ten days ago. My vision at distance is tremendous now.

I've had several injuries along the way but nothing major that affected my life. For instance, I dislocated my right thumb around the age of twelve. It kept popping out. I kept putting it back in but finally it's out and staying out. My grip on the right hand is a little weak. The major injury was the one I talked about earlier when describing work on the farm as a kid. I tore the major muscle in my right leg while operating that old hay rake.

This bothered me quite a bit. I couldn't run very fast, but we didn't do anything about it. We let it mend itself and it finally stopped hurting – but the leg never worked quite properly. Sometimes it would just collapse when I ran or worked hard. It prevented me from excelling even more than I did in several sports like track and field, football jumps and what have you. In skating I know that my right leg would drag once in a while and catch on the ice. Even in golfing lately, I've noticed that leg doesn't have the power you need.

Donna

I owe much of my success to my wife, Donna, who has been with me nearly fifty-nine years. When we were married, neither of us had really any worldly goods – we were young and immature – but Donna overlooked my shortcomings, coped with our poverty and shared in the good and bad times. Although she came from a background where most of life's needs were readily available, she dug in and made do with what little we had. She recovered from the terrible sadness of losing our first child and the knowledge that we would not have children of our own and, later, when we adopted our daughter and son she devoted herself to raising them, often on her own when my work took me away.

We seemed to have to paint every house we moved into and Donna not only painted but made curtains and whatever else was necessary to make it a home. She is a marvelous cook, and wherever we were located she presented a fine table. We were required to entertain often and she was a charming and gracious hostess and I was proud of her. She became an accomplished painter and friends and family have received her art. She became adept at decoupage to the extent that she sold some to Neiman Marcus! Donna's passion for antiques led us on many interesting quests which I must admit I enjoyed almost as much as she, and both we and our friends have enjoyed our "finds". She still plays both contract and duplicate bridge at a high level. Our life together has helped me immensely in my work. I have probably spent more time than most concentrating on my career with Esso. But Donna has been understanding and I know I could have not achieved what I have without her. Now that we are in our later years, maybe I can make an effort to contribute more time to a happy lifelong relationship.

Our children, Patricia and David, have traveled with us to my many postings around the world. This varied lifestyle gave them a world of experience. Tricia makes her home with us now and we are grateful for the help she provides us.

Trying to evaluate your lifetime of work and retirement – your life here on earth – is difficult. I've tried to do it a few

180

times but without any degree of success. Mine has been a really varied career – as you will have read. Every part of it has been interesting. Even the tough stuff I found rewarding. I wish I could have done more, especially in my athletics, but there's a limit to everything. You have only so much time and so much ability. It's been a wonderful life with many good people. I had a good upbringing – although it was a lot different from other people. But we seemed to turn out all right. I do think, though, that some of my early farm-related injuries hampered my athletics. I was always hopeful of getting to the Olympics but there weren't any held during wartime and, later, just trying to follow a career so as to be able to raise a family and support them got in the way. So, all in all, I'm pleased at the way it's gone, and I'm grateful for all the help I got from all the people I've known.

The End

Postscript (for my golfing friends!)

Some of the best golf I played was in England. I played a bit in the 1960s at the Malden Golf Club – not too far from Worcester Park. I could stop at the Malden station after work in London and walk to the course. I joined a bunch called the "Wreckers". I remember one game in the fog which was about as bad as it's ever been. We played seven holes in really thick fog. We would drive off and then fan out across the fairway and hope we could find the ball. In the 1980s I joined the Wentworth Golf Club. It was a great course with 45 holes – two 18's, east and west. The west course was the really tough one where they play all the competitions including, since 1964, the World's Match Play. That was the one year I went out and watched Arnold Palmer play.

Holes-in-one? My first was in 1982 at Wentworth. Three of us were playing the east course. It was blustery and rainy. We came to this shorter hole – about 165 yards. The wind was blowing from the left. I must have hit a slight draw because the ball held against the wind, landed about an inch right of the pin, flipped left with the draw spin and went in the hole. The second one was at Colwood after I retired, playing with three other buddies. Again there was nothing untoward about it – about 145 yards. After, I think I got a bottle and all the guys in the clubhouse got a drink. That was not like Wentworth. I had to buy my hole-in-one tie, so there wasn't much prize to that hole-in-one.

The third one was at the Richmond Golf Course just south of Vancouver. It was at a Pacific Northwest Seniors' Tournament. Jack Armitage and I entered as a team. At the beginning of the tournament they told us about this hole-in-one skin. You would put in a couple of dollars and the winner would take all. I didn't want to go in. There was a one-in-a-million chance of getting a hole-in-one. Jack said, "Come on, put your money in there," so we both went in. Later we came to this tough hole – about 190 yards. We all teed up and hit the ball. We weren't sure where any of them ended up. The front of the green seemed higher than the back. My ball went up there somewhere. We got up there and found their two and were looking for mine and couldn't find it. We looked all over, behind, around the side. All of a sudden Jack says, "Hey, wait a minute, here it is, it's in the hole." There it was, a 190-yard hole-in-one. I know I used a three-wood there. I won the low net and got another 253 dollars for the skin. I bought drinks for the group in front of us and the group behind (big deal!). We didn't stay for the prize-giving that evening as we had to catch a ferry back. But a couple of months later I got the money for the hole-in-one, a prize for the singles, and I think Jack and I won something for the doubles. That was a worthwhile hole-in-one. I think that was in 1993 and it's been a dry spell since. Its now '06 and I'm due, but chances of getting one now are getting slimmer and slimmer because my shots are getting wilder and wilder and not quite as near the pin all the time.

I think the best golf game I ever played was at Wentworth. I had joined there in 1980 and I didn't play much – only on Saturdays because nearly all my time was taken up by work. I think it was in July, 1983, and I entered the competition for what they called the Captain's Prize. It is considered the primary event of the year. The captain sets up the course the toughest way possible. This guy was an old Scottish captain and he made it really tough. He put the tees back as far as he could and put the pins in the worst positions he could think of. It was like an "iron man" kind of thing. Donna had gone to Paris to visit a friend for about three weeks so what I did was go from the office to the golf course. I had a bucket of balls in the car. There were four different practice areas at Wentworth and at that time of day they were not crowded. This meant I could practice my different shots on any of the four practice areas – driving, chipping, sand, wedge shots. I had about 100 balls in that bucket and probably hit about 400 or 500 every night for about three weeks.

On the day of the tournament there were about 155 of us playing. We played in threes. I played with complete strangers. We were the third group off in the morning. The 1st hole was a 471-yard par 4 with a big gully in front of the green. I hit a good drive, much better than my normal 250 or 260 yards. The second shot I hit pretty well with a three-wood, still 220 yards or more to the green, but I pushed it to the right and into the woods. I couldn't get a shot to the green so I went back sideways. I was three short of the green still, then chipped it on, then two-putted, so there I was with a double bogie right off the bat. I went then to the next hole, a short hole – 160 – got it on there, and two-putted for a three.

The next hole was a pretty tough par 4. It has a high green – very narrow – facing you. If you don't get up there the ball comes way back down the hill. I bogeyed that one. Next one was a par 5 – I parred that one. Next a long par 3, I parred that. I bogeyed 6 and 7, parred 8, and bogeyed 9. It went along like this – nothing tremendous. I finished the front 9 with a 41 – not too good after that initial double bogey. It was a par 35 on the front so I was 6 over. The 10th hole was somewhere around 200 yards and protected by some trees just in front of the green. It's kind of a tricky shot. I think I used the three and got on there about 8 feet away and darned if I didn't sink the putt (birdie). The next hole was a dog leg left par – 4,430 yards. I didn't do too well – on in three and three putts. The 12th hole, par 5, was probably the easiest to par and I did. The next, a par three, high green, again not too deep, wide, a tricky little shot. I got to the edge and got my three. The next hole was a long par 4, about 465 yards. I hit one about 280, put it on in 2 and 2 putted it. The next hole was a short par 4, dogleg left. I got it on and parred that one. Next a long par 5,571 yards. You drive from way up high. Then a dog leg left, hit it down – it landed in a little bit of rough on the right side. We looked there, couldn't find it, walked down a bit, and there it was 70 yards further and on the fairway. I hit that one with the three- wood, then 8-roned it on and two putted. The last hole was a shorter par 5,501 yards. I hit a reasonable drive, a reasonable second, a wedge on and, lo and behold, I sank the putt for a birdie. The back's a par 37 and I got a 38 on it. It was a tough back 9. Putting the two together it sounded pretty good but, considering there were 155 of us, with both gross and net and all the best golfers were there. Well, during the play the first two groups got into trouble and waved us through so we were the first group in. We signed our cards, handed them to the score keeper, then went into the bar and started enjoying ourselves. Well, a few minutes after, up comes the scorekeeper who whispers in my ear saying, "What are you doing tonight?" I said I don't know. "Why are you interested in what I'm doing tonight?" He says, "Because we think you've won." I asked how he could say I'd won when we were the first in. He said, "Well, we have experience with this, we know how the course is set up, so please – you should come." I said "OK, OK, I'll come." Well, it turned out that I had won the net by 5 strokes, I think it was. I was 5th best in the gross of all the better golfers so it was quite a round on that back 9. Anyway, I won the big trophy, got a little salver from the captain, and my name is on the Captain's board. There was room for only one more name. In the middle of two rows is "G.M. Hajash 43 Stableford." Then they started a new board.

That was the big event for that year. The next year we went into a couple of competitions and I was invited to the ceremonies after the Match Play in the fall where I met Greg Norman – he'd won the Match play that year ('84).

Another event we had at Wentworth in 1984 was the club's 60th anniversary celebration. We all dressed in '20s clothes. One fellow dressed as an aviator from WW1. I had a double-breasted suit and a big dark hat that made me look like a Mafioso. It was quite an evening. There were three orchestras. They didn't have enough room in the clubhouse so they set up a big marquee in the front with heaters and chandeliers.

There is another incident at Wentworth I still recall. Our foursome was playing along behind four captains. The captain and three former captains would get together on the Saturday morning to golf. Well, we got to this par 3 hole. We had just finished and could see that the captains' group ahead of us had been following another group. This group had stopped at the eat shack for breakfast. The rules say that, if no one is on the tee box, the next group plays through. Well, the captains' group teed up and a couple of guys came running out of the shack, yelling that they couldn't do that. They argued and the captains' group won. This animosity carried on for the remaining holes. When we got to the clubhouse again there was some discussion taking place at the cashier's wicket. Apparently the sponsor of the "bad" foursome had bought 3 tickets for the 9-hole course (you were not allowed to buy for the regular 18-hole course before 10 a.m. on Saturday). Now he wanted to be legit and pay the difference between the two. (I think he was asked to leave the Club.)

Appendices

Figure 17: Induction into University of Alberta Sports Wall of Fame, 1994.

Appendix 1
University of Alberta Sports Wall of Fame

Grayson Michael Hajash's life reads like an adventure novel. Born in northern Hungary, his family immigrated to Canada, living first in Estevan, Saskatchewan, and then on a farm near Brooks, Alberta. He graduated from Brooks high school in 1943. From his early school years in Canada, he excelled at hockey, softball, basketball and track and field, including a provincial record in the junior pole vault in 1941. At Alberta he had an outstanding career as a fullback and linebacker with the Golden Bears at a time when players went both ways, with very limited substitution. A feared runner, he was seldom denied in short yardage situations and his example and other leadership qualities led to his being made captain of the 1946 season, and to membership in the Block A Club. Meanwhile, he took part in intramurals in hockey, basketball, track and field and wrestling. In 1947 he was named winner of the Wilson Trophy as the outstanding male athlete on campus. He found time to serve terms as president of the Men's Athletic Board in 1946 /47 and the Track and Field Club in 1944/45 and in the summers suited up for the semi-pro Purity 99 baseball team, provincial champions in 1946. In 1947 Mickey earned a Bachelor of Science degree in Mining Engineering. After graduating he played the 1949 season with the Calgary Stampeder Football Club and since then has devoted his athletic efforts to golf. He has played on many of the most exotic courses in the world.

Mickey's professional working career began during summers of his undergraduate years in field exploration for Imperial Oil, a company with which he was to spend his entire working life. A deep concern for others is evident in a wide range of volunteer service beginning as a minor hockey coach in Edmonton in the late 1950s and, more recently, as a worker for the B.C. Games, international softball, senior golf, and preparations for the 1994 Commonwealth Games in Victoria. He was the moving force behind a 52-unit housing project for the needy and exceptional service to the United Way led to his nomination as Volunteer of the Year in 1993. Mindful of his roots, he and Donna have set up a foundation that at present is funding 8 post-secondary scholarships for graduates of Brooks Composite high school. Mickey Hajash has made a difference as a student and an athlete at Alberta and carried that quality forward into his family, professional and community life. [*University of Alberta newsletter article, author unknown.*]

***

THE HONOURABLE MR. JUSTICE
ALEXANDER ANDREKSON
THE LAW COURTS, EDMONTON, ALBERTA T5J 0R2
COURT OF QUEEN'S BENCH OF ALBERTA

November 15, 1993

Mr. Murray Smith
Chairman, Selection Committee 1135 Falconer Road
Edmonton, Alberta
T6R 2G6

Dear Murray:

Re: University of Alberta Sports Wall of Fame
GRAYSON MICHAEL (MICKEY) HAJASH

Further to my recent telephone call and your subsequent
letter, I am pleased and honoured to submit the name of
Mickey HAJASH for consideration by the Selection
Committee as a candidate for admission to the University of
Alberta Wall of Fame.

In support of the nomination, please find enclosed:

1. The curriculum vitae of the nominee;

2. A letter from C.E. Thiebaud (D.Sc.) Manager,
Exploration Division, Iraq Petroleum Company, Limited
with respect to a portion of his professional career in
various overseas operations, and the high regard for his
ability and achievements;

3. A letter from M.L. Van Vliet, retired head of the University of Alberta Physical Education Department and then coach of the Golden Bears Football Team; and

4. Outline of Sports and General Background.

Herb J. McLachlin was pleased to write a letter in support of Mickey's nomination. I have received a copy of such a letter.

In my respectful view, Mickey's athletic abilities and achievements are concisely chronicled in the enclosed curriculum vitae and the letters. It is my memory that the Wilson Trophy winner epitomized the highest honour that a male athlete could achieve at the University of Alberta. Without question, he was a deserving recipient of that Trophy.

Mickey has actively continued to participate in sports, particularly golf. While posted to the London, England head office of Iraq Petroleum Company, Mickey became a 5-year member of the Wentworth Golf Club. Members of your Selection Committee will know that the World Match Play Championships are played and have been played at Wentworth for the past 25 years (Corey Pavin having defeated Faldo on the last hole in 1993). In July 1983 Mickey won the Captain's Prize in Club Play Tournament by scoring a 79 (scratch at Wentworth being 74). His score was the 5th lowest gross score that day.

I thought your Committee would be interested in further details concerning the Continuing Education Foundation that Donna and Mickey established in 1990 for the benefit of one male and one female student graduating each year from the Brooks Consolidated High School with aspirations of continuing their post secondary education. It is an open competition whereby all graduating students can apply. The criteria utilized by the teaching staff in its selection process and mandated by the bylaws of the Foundation are threefold; academic excellence, high athletic achievement and active participation in student and community affairs. The winners each receive a $1,500.00 grant for each year that they attend and continue their education, for up to four years at any university or college of the recipient's choice. At the present time there are eight recipients, each of whom are receiving their $1,500.00 grant from the Foundation. One of the recipients was Jonene Schalm who enrolled in Physical Education at the University of Alberta and played on the Panda Basketball Team for three years.

Mickey was awarded the Victoria Volunteer of the Year Award from United Way in 1993. He has volunteered his services to the upcoming Commonwealth Games which are to be held in Victoria in 1994.

Naturally, it is my hope that the Committee will give its favourable consideration to Mickey, whom I consider to be an outstanding, deserving nominee. If there is further information required, please call me at 422-2403 (Court House) or 434-9010 (home) or write to 29 Westbrook Drive, Edmonton T6J 2C8.

Thank you for your consideration.

Yours truly,

A. Andrekson

***

Mr. Justice A. Andrekson
29 Westbrook Drive
Edmonton, Alberta
T5N 2S7

November 27, 1992

Dear Andy:

It is with great pleasure that I write in support of the nomination of Mr. Grayson Hajash (Mickey) to be a member of the University of Alberta Sports Wall of Fame. I know of no one who is better qualified to be considered for this honor.

As an undergraduate Mr. Hajash was an outstanding member of the Block A Club, having been a "star" on the track team and Captain of the Track Club. As a member of the football team he was a western collegiate all-star. In the year 1946-47 he was the winner of the Wilson Trophy which is presented to the most outstanding athlete in the university. During this period he was also the President of University Athletic Boar

Others will provide more detailed information concerning Mr. Hajash's many accomplishments. As one who was directly involved with the athletic program at the University of Alberta for over 40 years I merely wish to state that he was and is one of Alberta's all-time "Greats". What is perhaps much more important is the fact that he has distinguished himself in his profession and has made numerous contributions of scholarships to high school students. He has also been extremely active in fund-raising.

It is an honor for me to recommend Mr. Hajash as worthy candidate for membership in the University of Alberta Sports Wall of Fame.

Sincerely yours, (Sgd. M. L. Van Vliet)

***

5815 114A St.
Edmonton, T6H 3M8
Nov. 9/93

Re: Grayson Michael "Mickey" Hajash
Dear Murray

I had a call from Andy Andrekson asking if I would write a letter re Mickey Hajash who he is proposing for induction into the Sports Wall of Fame.

I am most pleased to do so and upon reviewing Mickey's athletic achievements I was reminded of his outstanding contributions to Golden Bear Teams. The Selection Committee will no doubt have a record of his accomplishments. As a former Intramural Director, it gave me pleasure to note that he was also a participant in the interfaculty program in basketball and wrestling.

His receiving of the Block "A" Award in 1945 and the awarding of the Wilson Challenge Trophy a year later certainly indicates that he joined a very special group of university athletes.

A few years ago, in Victoria, I had the pleasure of golfing with Mickey at his home course at the Royal Colwood.

A gracious host and an excellent golfer he took it easy on such "hackers" as Ted Sawchuk, Maury Van Vliet and myself. It was here for a number of reasons "I got to know" that Mickey Hajash deserves the title of sportsman.

Upon reviewing names of previous inductees into the sports Wall of Fame, I can think of no one who is more deserving.

Without reservations, if asked, I would fully support the nomination of Mickey Hajash. He deserves very serious consideration.

Sincerely,
Sgd. H. J. McLachlin

***

Acceptance Speech by Mickey Hajash

Mr. Chairman, honoured guests, students, alumni and friends, it's a great honour to say a few words on behalf of the inductees of 1994. All four of us reached the same goal, we started at the same place, university, but each one of us had a different route to get there. In the next few minutes or so I'd like to tell you how I got there. First of all it's been a wonderful life, and I have lots to thank for it. First thanks to this great nation of ours, accepting our family into this country, to become citizens to be integrated in the community and to live and work in peace and harmony in this nation. Second, for this great education system we have. I know this week they've been debating it and saying maybe it isn't that good, but I think it's tremendous and for me it culminated in a degree from U of A, and for that I'm very thankful. I thank my teachers, coaches, friends, fellow students, alumni for preparing me for a very interesting, adventuresome and rewarding career, but the university did more than that, it prepared me for after that, it taught me how to care for people, work with people and to help them. My involvement in team sports, with football hockey basketball, baseball and fastball in the summer season taught me to work with others, help each other, we relied on each other to achieve the ultimate goal. My well I think it mentioned on the film that I enjoyed blocking more than scoring a touch down, to me the ultimate wasn't to score the touchdown, it was to knock two down during the play, that was my big goal .In baseball it was not the homerun or the spectacular catch, it was getting on base; heckling the heck out of the pitcher and making it easier for my following batters to get on base, that was the fun. My involvement in the track and field club, the men's athletic board taught me how to work with people especially in committees, how to help people. I spent four years in the Rutherford House, as a D U. they were very four formative years and I thank my fellow brothers for help and guidance in forming my character.

It was a tremendous experience, but to go on from there it prepared me for after my career. I have been deeply involved in caring for the needy in the community as you heard on the video; I'm involved with the United Way and have been for years. In addition, with my wife's help, and the private foundation we have we are making it possible for eight young Albertans to get a university education, in addition to that stuff I'm involve with anything that comes along that is worthy, currently I'm working with the Commonwealth Games preparations and you know we're going to have eleven days of real excitement out there, and if you don't know when it is, its August 18th-August 28th and we hope to see some of you out there.

Now I'd like to mention that one of my students, one of our first scholarship winners is here tonight, and Jeneen would you stand up; she's graduating this year from University of Alberta. Now with all this forgoing lets not forget though where we came from and who helped us, and we must remember to support our university, to make sure that they can maintain that high level of education and campus life that we enjoyed and brought us here tonight; a thank you to the university. Go on from there to this evening, I'm speaking for all four of the inductees now, and we have many people to be thankful for. First of all our nominators, and our sponsors we thank them for their faith in us and for the many good things they've said about us. Then to the panel, the Wall of Fame panel, for their sorting out fact from fiction, and choosing several candidates out of many worthy ones. Then we must remember friends, teachers, past and present, who for some reason or other could not be here, and we'll remember them in our hearts and our thoughts, there are a lot of them who would have been here if it was possible. Last of all we want to thank the organizing committee for this evening, they had a minimum amount of time this year, as you can imagine, and a minimum budget and they did a tremendous job. Now in addition, I'd like to thank all of you for being here and sharing this evening with and for supporting the university that made it all possible. Thank You.

***

Harvard University
Graduate School of Business Administration

J. R. S. Jorgens
#2 139ll 16 Ave.
White Rock, BC
V4A 1P8
Dec. 30/94

To my dear friend "Mickey" Grayson Michael Hajash:

Congratulations on your election to the U of A "Sports Wall of Fame" which was duly deserved by your athletic record.

But even more congratulations are due on the excellent quality of your speech on behalf of yourself and other inductees, and the dignified delivery before cameras with ready script.

Your choice of words, composition, and delivery, clearly indicates your dedication to the hard work of careful preparation.

I am most proud to be one of your DU brothers in such illustrious company as yourself.

With best wishes for improving health and strengthening that "big, big" heart.

May the winds of good fortune be with you always.

Sincerely,
(Sgd) Jack

***

Appendix II
12th Annual Community Awards 1995 CFAX Community Awards

Citizen Of The Year: Mickey Hajash

Mickey Hajash is an incredible volunteer, says Margo McLaren Moore, Director of Campaign and Development at the United Way. He is always ready to roll up his sleeves.

Born in Hungary, Hajash has lived all over the world, coming to Canada at age 5 and growing up in Alberta. He shone as an athlete, achieving Hall of Fame status and the Wilson trophy as a university track and field star and playing for the Calgary Stampeders for a year. Then his work in the oil business demanded his time, sending the family to such far-off places as Baghdad, Kuala Lumpur and England.

"Mickey always wanted to come to Victoria", says his wife Donna. "Now we're here and we love it".
A volunteer for over five years with the United Way, Hajash has the ability to charm dollars out of the tightest pockets. This year alone he raised over $140,000 for the cause. And has been actively raising significant amounts each year of his involvement. Hajash served on the Board of Directors, and as a liaison to the Single Parents Resource Centre, but due to a recent heart attack has had to resign many of his duties. He hopes to be back again when recovery permits.

He organizes the Superannuates Campaign each year, an important fund raiser among retirees from Imperial Oil and Esso. During the Commonwealth Games, Hajash served as Attaché to the trouble-plagued Sierra Leone team. "It was a lot of work, but exciting", says Donna. Hajash's life-long interest in athletics also prompted him to volunteer for the BC Games.

Hajash has put his experience, and his compassion and caring to excellent use for the benefit of Victoria citizens and is truly deserving of the Merit Award of the Year.

***

Appendix III

Albert Fia, Mickey's mentor at high school in Brooks went on to become a major figure in Canadian aerospace research and development.

Mr. Albert Fia   [Legislative Assembly of Manitoba, Wednesday, June 9th 2004.]

Mr. Ralph Eichler (Lakeside): Today is a sombre day, as the man known as the father of Canadian rocketry is no longer with us. Albert Fia passed away at the age of 89 on Saturday, June 5, at the Grace Hospice.

Born in Lethbridge, Alberta, in 1915, Albert Fia later went on to marry Kathleen Baldwin in Brooks, Alberta, who was serving as principal of the local school. Albert attended the Royal Military College of Science in England and Laval University, where he earned his engineering degree.

After serving in the Second World War and the military for many years, Albert left the army in 1958 to take a position with Bristol Aerospace in Manitoba as director of the aerospace program. His work at Bristol in the early 1960s led to the development of the Black Brant rocket. The Black Brant rocket series became one of the most successful solid propellant upper atmosphere research rockets used by scientists in Europe, the United Kingdom and the United States.

Fia retired in 1980 as vice-president of Bristol Aerospace, but his legacy lives on. The Brant rockets are still used for research by NASA as well as other universities and government agencies in the United States and around the world.

Since 1962 more than 800 Black Brants have been launched around the world, contributing to a greater understanding of space and putting Manitoba on the map for bringing such a valuable export to the world. After his retirement, Fia was greatly honoured when he received the Public Service Award from NASA for his work on Brant rockets, which was the first of its kind ever awarded to a citizen of another country other than the United States.

Mr. Speaker, Albert Fia was an exceptional member of our business and science community. We greatly miss his presence. My condolences go out to his family and many friends at this difficult time.

***

Appendix IV

Letter of Recommendation from Dr. Thiebaud of the IPC.
IRAQ PETROLEUM COMPANY, LIMITED
33 CAVENDISH SQUARE LONDON WI   TELEPHONE
MAYFAIR 9405

TELEGRAMS   Inland PETRIRAQ   TELEX   LONDON
Foreign PETRIRAQ LONDON W.I.   Code Bentley's
SECOND PHRASE

EXP/67 /27 3rd February, 1967

Chief Geophysicist - G.M. Hajash

I testify in my capacity of Manager, Exploration
Division, of the Iraq Petroleum and Associated Companies
at the headquarters of our Group, in London; our overseas
operations are in Iraq, Qatar and Abu Dhabi.

Mr. Hajash was seconded to us as Senior Geophysicist
in May 1960 from one of our Shareholders, Standard Oil
Company of New Jersey, with whom he had then been
associated for 14 years.

He served in Iraq for two years attached to our main
office in Baghdad. In March 1962 he went to Bahrain, also
as Senior Geophysicist, in preparation for his transfer to
London where, in May 1963, he became Chief
Geophysicist, the highest geophysical office in our Group of
Companies.

He has remained in this post until now.

A very competent, hard-working geophysicist, he has
been responsible for a most impressive series of
achievements in our operations which, very largely due to

204

his remarkable ability, can be regarded as very outstanding. Facing the constantly rising costs of seismic work he has nevertheless managed, in 1966, to cut the cost per unit, the km, by some 20% on the average cost of the six previous years, 1960-1965, and this in spite of using more elaborate methods - therefore more costly - which have resulted in an improved quality of the work produced.

He has been active in other fields of exploration and more generally his knowledge of the problems of the whole oil industry has been a very useful asset to us. He has often acted as my Deputy.

He has been nominated to present a very important paper to the World Petroleum Congress in Mexico in April 1967. This paper, on the geology of Abu Dhabi, relates the story of a successful exploration for oil: oil production which started in 1964 was last week at a rate of 300,000 b/d. The role played by Mr. Hajash in this venture has been important.

He is an inspiration to all his colleagues and although he was offered posts with higher responsibility he has chosen to return to the Jersey Group.

A man of disciplined taste, pleasant with all; his departure is very much regretted.

(C. E. Thiebaud) D .Sc.
Manager,
Exploration Director

***

SIERRA INVEST TRADING CO. (SL) LTD.

26, Siaka Stevens Street,
Freetown,
Sierra Leone
West Africa.
19th. September, 1994

Ref:
Tel: 225544
Fax: 225937

G. M. Hajash,
3160 Ripon Road, Victoria, B.C V8R665,
British Columbia, Canada.

Dear Mickey,

I am sorry that it has taken so long for me to write to you but I did not return home until last Sunday, as I spent an extra week in London trying to recuperate after the hectic time at the Games. The Flight to London was quite exhausting and I just needed the rest.

On my return I received a letter from an Anglican Priest in Victoria, who attended my school and made contact with me through your usual good auspices. It was a most reassuring letter and helped me to explain to my people here that the British Columbians were too sympathetic to our cause and had gone out of their way to make our stay in Victoria a memorable one.

In this regard, I want to once more formally thank you for all you did for us. In all my travels to Games around the

World, I have never met with an Attache who got himself so involved with not only our successes, but also problems and failures - you were part and parcel of everything that concerned us - as a result you smiled with us and symbolically wept with us in times of grief.

I do not know how I will be able to repay your kindnesses and I am just hoping that I will be able to be successful in getting a Twinning Relationship between our two Cities. If that can be achieved, I hope that it will be possible for you to be included in the party from Victoria for the Ceremony here. You should be there as you have played a major role in making us feel at home in your beautiful and clean City.

I will never forget your contribution in uplifting me during the periods when I experienced the lowest ebbs of my career. Thank you, may God grant you continued wealth and strength in your retirement - more important still, peace of mind.

Please remember me to your wife and family,

Yours Sincerely,

J.B. Benka – Coker

End of Appendices